AGNOSTICISM IS ALSO FAITH

by the same author:

The Life and Teaching of Lucius Annaeus Seneca

AGNOSTICISM IS ALSO FAITH

George G. Strem, Ph.D.
Professor Emeritus
California State University, Chico

First Edition

Library of Congress Catalog No. 85-90970

Copyright © 1986 by George G. Strem

Libra Publishers, Inc.
4901 Morena Blvd.
Suite 330
San Diego, California 92117

Manufactured in the United States of America

ISBN 0-87212-194-1

To the memory of Spinoza, my Master.

CONTENTS

AGNOSTICISM IS ALSO FAITH

Chapter I

RELIGION

When human beings first began to be aware of themselves in relation to the world around them, they realized that they were dependent upon forces beyond their control. The sun, the climate, the nature of the soil, an abundance or lack of water and other factors could provide them with a good life or else destroy them. To propitiate these powerful forces they offered up sacrifices. To primitive man, the struggle for survival meant to kill or be killed, so it was not unnatural that he should offer human sacrifice to the gods. These gods were depicted in a frightful manner as both hideous and malevolent.

The moloch was an iron statue which was heated until incandescent. Then it swallowed up the young men and women thrown into its jaws. Virgins were often cast into rivers or lakes where the god that lived there supposedly would take possession of them.

As time passed, mortals became more benign and the gods were also imagined to be more gentle. Human sacrifices were replaced by animals, food, flowers or other gifts. Man's concept of his divinities was altered by changes in society.

The Greeks imagined their gods to be just like themselves, except that they possessed greater powers. They were believed to live on Mount Olympus, where they enjoyed divine food and drink. They were not immune to passions such as jealousy and anger. Sometimes they intervened in human affairs or even mingled with human beings.[1]

The Romans, who were great imitators, adopted Greek mythology, giving Latin names to these divinities. They carved

1

images of the gods and placed them in their temples, where it was convenient to conciliate them with flattering words whispered in their ears, or to bribe them by slipping money into their garments. They also adopted other foreign gods such as Oriental divinities and established their special rites and ceremonies.

In Asia, two main religions sprang up: Brahmanism and Buddhism. Brahmanism condemned a large number of people to lifetime servitude, for its doctrine holds that the ancestors of such people have committed abominable crimes for which their descendants must atone. These poor unfortunates form a caste known as "the untouchables." It is claimed that if even the shadow of one of these should fall upon a Brahman, it would contaminate him. Because it is cloaked in religion, this heartless doctrine is certain of acceptance by its victims. Thus, cheap labor and obedience is guaranteed to the masters.

Today, the untouchables are legally emancipated, but in practice, this doctrine still prevails in innumerable rural communities of India.

Buddhism is now losing its force on the subcontinent. Its strength has shifted to Ceylon (today Sri Lanka), Thailand, China, and other countries. But it is gaining adherents in Europe and is finding even more converts in the United States. This religion, which is the most important one in Asia, preaches charity, compassion and the brotherhood of man, but requires renunciation of sensual pleasures. It teaches the doctrine of the Karma, namely, that the merits or demerits of our ancestors determine the shape and station in which we are born, and that we are reborn eternally until the Self is cleansed of all ambition and desire, thus attaining the bliss of the Nirvana, that complete serenity which no emotion can disturb. This doctrine implies that life is a penance. Buddhism is hostile to life, which makes it a negative religion. If all mankind were to follow its tenets, the human race would become extinct. Buddhism leads to the decline of material prosperity, to inaction. It is all very well for the Buddhist monks to beg for their food, but that food must be produced by farmers' labor, and some other worker must weave their saffron robes.

Today, the majority of mankind professes one of four religions: Buddhism, Judaism, Christianity or Islam. Judaism, in its orthodoxy, holds that the Jews received their religious tenets from God through the agency of their prophet, Moses. This conviction, that they have a covenant with God, is at the very core of Jewish faith, and, in fact, of Jewish consciousness. To them, it signifies that they are the Chosen People, and this belief has enabled them to endure persecution for the last two thousand years. The Jews feel different from other people and other people feel that they are indeed different. Their singularity lies in the fact that they were the first to proclaim monotheism, or One God, the Creator of the Universe. This idea was unheard of, and incomprehensible to the ancient world, which was accustomed to the worship of many gods.

The fact that the Jews are certain that they are the Chosen People explains their fierce resistance to Roman conquest. But in the end their temple and their capital were destroyed and they themselves dispersed throughout the Roman empire. In captivity, they made themselves conspicuous by refusing to work on the Sabbath. Saint Augustine, in *The City of God,* quotes Seneca (without giving any reference), concerning this custom of the Jews, saying that they act uselessly in keeping those seventh days, thereby they use through idleness about the seventh part of their life, and also many things which demand immediate attention.

And Seneca, as quoted by Saint Augustine, adds: "Meanwhile the custom of that most accursed nation has gained such strength that they have been now received in all lands, the conquered have given laws to the conquerors."[2] Pondering the holy scriptures, listening to and living for God, the orthodox Jew is present in the flesh only; his is the spiritual realm. Since the creation of a Jewish nation in Israel, a new generation of Jews have renounced their messianic mission, and desire to be like every other nation. This has made those cling-

3

ing to the old faith feel like exiles, as their ancestors did during the dispersion; and they fear that this abandonment of tradition will result in the loss of the Jewish cultural heritage.

Judaism inspired both Christianity and Islam. Each borrowed some tenets from Judaism and reveres some of its prophets.

The basic tenets of Christianity are:

That Jesus, son of God, took upon himself the sins of all mankind and died upon the cross to save us. That the godhead is threefold, consisting of Father, Son, and Holy Ghost. The Council of 325 A.D. formulated the dogma of the Holy Trinity as follows: "These three are one true eternal God, the same in substance, equal in power and glory, although distinguished by their personal properties."[3]

The consubstantiation of the Christ with the Father was denied by the Arian sect, which led to bloody persecution and the eventual eradication of Arianism.

Christianity shares with Judaism a belief in the spiritual essence of man, which is part of God's own essence. It also emphasizes that true bliss can be found only in heaven; that this life is a vale of tears, its purpose being that man should live so as to deserve salvation.

The implication here is similar to the Buddhist feeling that life is sinful and man must atone for it. Such a belief stems from the doctrine of original sin.

Indeed, Saint Augustine's major work, *The City of God,* says this:

> God . . . was pleased to derive all men from one individual, and created man with such a nature that the members of the race should not have died, had not the two first (of whom the first was created out of nothing, and the other out of him) merited this by their disobedience; for by them so great a sin was committed that by it the human nature was altered for the worse, and was transmitted also to their posterity, liable to sin and subject to death.[4]

4

And in his *Confessions* he maintains that even babies can commit sins. "It is clear, indeed, that infants are harmless because of physical weakness, not because of any innocence of mind. I myself have seen and known a baby who was envious; it could not yet speak, but it turned pale and looked bitterly at another baby sharing its milk ... Can one really describe as 'innocence' the conduct of one who, when there is a fountain of milk flowing richly and abundantly, would not allow another child to have his share of it, even though this other child is in the greatest need and indeed in this stage depends entirely on this nourishment to keep alive?"[5]

The greatest of the church fathers did not know that psychology and law recognize responsibility only when one can tell the good from evil, which the baby he spoke of obviously could not do yet.

Without this doctrine of the original sin, there would have been no need for a Redeemer; the crucifixion of Jesus would have been pointless.

Islam arose in the last third of the sixth century A.D. and is therefore a much newer religion than either Judaism or Christianity. Its prophet was a simple camel driver in Arabia who was possessed with a holy zeal, as was Jesus six centuries earlier. He preached to pagan Arabs about an invisible, all-powerful God whom he called Allah. Muhammat or Mohammed, as he called himself, borrowed ideas from both Judaism and Christianity and adapted these to the character of the Arab people, to their way of life, their hopes and aspirations. Mohammed had it in him to become a great military commander, so religion was made to serve military aspirations and was, in fact, his most formidable weapon. He persuaded his men that if they died in battle, they would awaken to find themselves in a shady arbor, surrounded by beautiful, passionate maidens. These virgins would offer the men delicious food and drink, as well as their delectable bodies.

The promise of such a future life was simple enough for even

5

the most primitive to understand. It made his soldiers what he wanted them to be, men who would risk any danger with no regard for their own survival. This is one explanation for the amazing success of his armies on the field of battle. In less than a decade, they had conquered the Arab peninsula and laid the foundation of a new world empire. Islam had achieved by the sword what Christianity had accomplished with the Word, namely, a world religion which has endured to this day. In this last quarter of the 20th Century, Islam has shown a new aggressiveness. The ruthless way in which young lives are sacrificed by the hundreds of thousands in the war between two Muslim countries, Iran and Iraq, demonstrates once again the warlike character of this religion.

The Koran, which is the holy book of Islam, contains one commandment which is identical to that which Moses gave the Jews: OBEY GOD! The Koran contains no theology; it is only a manual of conduct, giving rules about marriage, and religious rites such as facing Mecca during the daily prayer, or abstaining from food in the daytime during the month of Ramadan. It even rules on the positions that are proper during sexual intercourse. It contains no great literature such as we find in the Bible.

The Koran codifies the superiority of men over women. No other religious or philosophical work, nor any civilized set of laws has ever segregated the sexes so strictly. Woman is man's servant, nay, man's property, which means that she is virtually a slave. A man may have four wives if he can afford them, and he may repudiate any of them by the use of a certain formula. It is true that the Koran admonishes man to treat his wife kindly, but she is utterly dependent upon his good will; indeed, woman's status in the Islamic household is similar to that of a pet animal in the Western world.

Arab and other Muslim women who, earlier in the century, had begun to insist upon emancipation, are now returning to the fold, either voluntarily or because they are forced to. An article published in the *Los Angeles Times* on December 16, 1982 makes this statement:

Arab women are still more segregated and less liberated than any other women in the world. The Arab woman is expected first to be obedient to her husband—who may have three other wives, any of whom he can easily divorce. The Koran, the Muslim holy book, defines the woman's role as essentially biological. The claims that Islam is a progressive religion that gave women their rights, liberating them more than other religions, simply does not stand the test of reality.[6]

The article was written by Mona Abousenna, a Muslim feminist scholar at Al Shams University in Cairo.

Egypt is today the most progressive of all the Arab countries in its laws and customs concerning women. And yet, women who go to medical school in Cairo attend separate classes and refuse instruction dealing with some aspects of the male anatomy. Mosques and even mausoleums are segregated. In Algiers' City Hall there are two windows for paying bills, one for men and one for women. Although it is one of the principal cities in Algeria, a country which prides itself on being socialist and progressive, it would seem that even here religious and social traditions prevail over ideology.

The birth of an Arab boy is cause for great celebration, and boys are nursed longer than girls because a woman gains status in her husband's family by producing sons. A woman who commits adultery is stoned to death and her lover is also killed. Recently a film entitled "Death of a Princess" was shown on the American network, CBS. It was about a young woman belonging to the royal family of Saudi Arabia, who had committed adultery. She was put to death and her lover was beheaded. This film aroused consternation in both the United States and Europe.

There is a revival of the most extreme fanaticism going on in the Islamic world of today. It began in 1979 with the overthrow of the Shah of Iran. Those liberal politicians who had contributed to the success of the revolution were under attack soon after for their political views and were forced to flee. One of them, named Gobzadeh, who had been a longtime friend of the Ayatollah Komeini, religious leader of the revolution, was

7

beheaded. The mullahs, or clergy, of Islam, have taken over all positions of power. Iran is openly attempting to spread Islamic fundamentalism among Muslims everywhere. This aggressive movement fosters unrest, supports terrorism, and constitutes a grave menace to peace in the Middle East. Islam is today, as it was in Muhammet's time, a political and warlike religion.

The Balance Sheet of Religion

BENEFITS OF RELIGION

Alliance between Church and State
In the year 800, Charlemagne became Emperor of the "Holy Roman Empire of the German Nation," a political entity which endured for a thousand years. It was the Roman Pope who placed the crown upon his head, thus forming an alliance between the Church and the ruler of the strongest nation on the continent. It was the fusion of worldly and spiritual power. Henceforth, kings could claim to reign *Deo gratia,* by the grace of God. In return, the Church was protected by the sword of the King. Even more important was the fact that a concept of universals was born: one King, one Church, and one Empire. This concept inspired Charlemagne with the determination to convert all of his subjects to Christianity, even by force if necessary. He understood the unifying and cohesive powers of the Church and the ability of religion to civilize his nation.

Resting Once a Week
The alliance between Church and State bore fruit in the life of the peasant as well as the population in general. Charlemagne issued an edict, which was later upheld by his successors, specifying that one day a week be set aside on which no work should be done except that which was absolutely necessary. This edict, which conforms to the Tenth Commandment and was prompted by the Church, freed the serf every seventh

day and on holidays. For one day the peasant could find rest, and not only for his body; his mind, too, could rest in the assurance that he also had rights, and was part of the great human community of Christians. Indeed, the Emperor's edict had stated: "Let them come together from all sides to mass in the Church, and praise God for all good things He did for us on that day."[7]

Work itself acquired more meaning from then on, for man ceased to be a beast of burden and became a child of God, and while he served his master, he also felt he served the Lord. The Church was to him a shelter where he could forget life's toil and hardship, and the poorest man could take comfort in the fact that all are equal in the sight of God. The Church was a pleasant place too, filled with voices raised in song. The plainchant, which consisted of tunes sung in unison by the priest and congregation, created a bond between them, a feeling of belonging. Music endeared the Church to people; the chant, the choir and the organ created harmonies which worshippers took with them when the services were over.

Religion provided an alternative to the tavern. Emerging from church, the people in their Sunday best, still hearing echoes of that solemn concord of which they had been a part, were loath to break the spell by going to a public house. Instead, they sang and danced within the churchyard.

Inspiration for the Arts

In Europe up until the Renaissance, religion had been the principal source of inspiration for the arts. There were many legends about the Holy Family, and about saints and miracles. These inspired painters for generations. Churches were decorated with paintings of Biblical events. These pictures expressed the piety, the desire for transcendence, and religious fervor of the artists.

The greatest religious story of all, the Passion of Christ and his crucifixion, offered an abundance of themes to be enacted, thus laying the foundation of a theatrical art. Passion plays,

9

such as those which the Bavarian town of Oberammergau has made famous, became a yearly event. Every member of the community played some role, and these events attracted countless visitors throughout the centuries. Literature was enriched by the narration of these significant religious events. Music too, was greatly benefited by religious inspiration. Western civilization has a rich heritage of Christian church music.

Statues were erected both inside and outside of churches, honoring local saints. These figures sometimes depicted scenes from their lives, and in this way, even the illiterate could become acquainted with religious history. These lifelike images inspired the faithful with personal affection for their saints. Individuals had favorite saints to whom they would appeal in time of trouble. Every trade union, or guild, as they were called, had its own patron saint whom its members could call upon to intercede for them. Images of these saints were accompanied by emblems, which made them easy to recognize. Pictures of saints were given to young people when they were confirmed and at family festivals. Sometimes they were awarded for good moral behavior.

This personal and affectionate regard which people had for their saints gave sweetness and intimacy to the act of worship. Religion, as we said earlier, fostered a sense of belonging. It became indispensable to men's well-being, a safe harbor where they could take shelter from the storms of life and find renewal.

The development of European architecture, as well as music, was due mainly to Chirstianity. The massive Romanesque gave way to a new and more graceful type of construction. Flying buttresses on the exterior of the church permitted the elimination of walls between points where the thrust was concentrated, and allowed for their replacement with glass. Vertical treatment plus the elimination of unnecessary structural features gave it a more delicate and ethereal appearance. The pointed arch was a symbol of prayer, the pillars, the nave and the towers rose boldly on narrow supports. And, thanks to the invention of stained glass, the interior was softly illuminated.

The magnificent cathedrals in Chartres, Reims, Beauvais and Bruges, not to mention Notre Dame in Paris and many others, were a triumph of human ingenuity as well as being great works of art. They were also a testimony to the religious devotion of the people, for some of these cathedrals took centuries to build. Wars, epidemics, all kinds of disasters interrupted their construction, and sometimes they were finished by anonymous artisans, humble but skillful men, who donated time after their regular work, with no other compensation than the satisfaction of using their artistry to glorify God. But the most exquisite of European cathedrals can hardly compare to the splendor and architectural beauty of certain Oriental temples.

During the early Middle Ages, when few people knew how to read or write, monasteries were seats of learning. Monks cultivated the art of embellishing the manuscripts which they were copying from ancient texts. They illuminated the first word of every paragraph using specially treated colored inks. And each letter of the word was gracefully formed. These exquisite manuscripts were an ornament to any library.

Confession and Absolution of Sins

Confession, which brought absolution and the promise of salvation, was probably Catholicism's greatest gift to the faithful. Hearts that were heavy with guilt and remorse could find relief through the confessional. Kneeling before it, speaking to an invisible person as one would to God, the faithful could unload their burden. The penitence imposed upon them was a small price to pay for the euphoria which confession induced. They felt cleansed and renewed, reconciled with God and grateful for His mercy, ready to begin again. The Church helped people to live with themselves. And it helped them to die. Extreme unction, or the last sacrament, was administered by the priest, who recited with them, or for them, the prayer of the dying. Christian burial gave dignity to their departure and offered solace to the survivors in the belief that their loved ones would continue life in a spiritual realm beyond the grave.

Today, as in the past, religion is a deep-felt need for a vast number of people, and a potent force in shaping the destinies of nations. Even in countries whose constitutions profess to be nonreligious, the attraction of religion has not died out. In Poland, for example, the power of the Church parallels that of the state, and it is interesting to note that the American preacher, Billy Graham, attracted great crowds of people, both young and old, when he was in Hungary and the Soviet Union. The Roman Catholic Pope's visits to foreign countries, even to Marxist ones, draw hundreds of thousands of people. In the United States we find that modern technology has become the servant of religion. People from all walks of life donate enormous sums to the so-called electronic churches, listening to their sermons on television and on radio.

Religion Offers Transcendence
The secret of religion's abiding power lies in the human yearning for transcendence which it offers. Man clings to the hope that there is something more, something beyond this brief life on earth, so full of pain and struggle, with its fleeting joys and bitter disillusion. He dreams of eternity, of an unending spiritual existence. Man is the only creature on this planet who knows his life to be but a short interlude in the eternal unfolding of the universe, and he cannot resign himself to this inexorable fact. Religion denies the extinction of the conscious "I"; it offers hope that an eternal Being, loving and compassionate, is always at hand. Though dwelling in the realm of spirit, He is ever aware of us and will protect and guide us to fulfillment. Religion has been invented by man in order to make life tolerable.

No Racial or Class Prejudice
One of Catholicism's greatest attractions is that it ignores racial and class differences. During the first century of the Roman Empire, Christians were forced to hide out in the catacombs. They received those who wished to join them with open

arms; whether they were slaves or members of the Roman aristocracy made no difference. All were treated as equals. Roman Catholicism has never made any distinction among its adherents, whatever their race or social status. Thus, during the Middle Ages the only way to overcome the restrictions of the feudal system was to embrace the priesthood. Any member of the clergy could expect to reach the highest rank in the hierarchy, if his talent and dedication to the faith warranted it. The catholic character of the Church required that priests be recruited from among all races and classes. There have been black bishops and cardinals—Saint Augustine was an African; today's Archbishop of Paris was born of Jewish parents who were deported by the German Nazis and perished in a concentration camp. Their son was baptized and educated by the Church.

THE DARK SIDE OF RELIGION

As we have noted, religion is a vital and sustaining force which gives solace to the disfranchised and unfortunate. It helps people to live and die with peace of mind. It has, however, a dark side. Religion has been the cause of untold human suffering, and many abominable crimes have been committed in its name. When we draw up a balance sheet as to the good and bad effects of organized religion, we find the bad far outweighs the good in spite of the numerous benefits we have mentioned.

Religion Is Divisive

Religion does bring people together, but ultimately it is divisive. The history of Christianity is replete with dissension, schisms and fratricidal strife, from the establishment of the Roman Church in the first century A.D., up to the present day. Dogmas of the Church were challenged as early as the third century by followers of Arius. In the fourth century, they were opposed by the Manicheans, to whom even St. Augustine had

13

adhered in his youth. They were followed by other reformers, the principal ones being: Wyclif in England, his disciple, John Huss in Bohemia, and Martin Luther, whose 95 theses (affixed to the church door in Wittenberg) set off a conflagration which could not be put out.

The division between Catholics and Protestants continues to this day. In addition to this major schism, Protestantism has developed a wide variety of separate denominations. Walk through any American town and you will come across such names as "The Assembly of God," "The Church of God," and "The Church of the Nazarene." Then there are the large and well known denominations, such as Methodist, Presbyterian, Baptist, and Congregational. Taken as a whole, though, Protestants feel somewhat distant from Catholics, and the Jews, who are felt to be a breed apart, do not mingle much with gentiles. Judaism, too, is made up of various groups: the orthodox versus the reformed church, and the Eastern, or Sephardi, versus Western or Ashkenazi Jews. We find that Buddhism also has variations. It is practiced differently in Tibet than it is in Sri Lanka, Thailand, and other countries.

These large schisms, as well as endless minor ones within the larger groups, have led to frightful slaughter around the world, and brought untold misery in their wake. Religion's goal, namely the elevation of the human race, has been made the pretext for cruelty and oppression.

The Constitution of the United States was written by men who were well aware of this danger. They had the wisdom to stipulate that there should be no established religion in America—that church and state must be forever separate.

Of Religious Intolerance

The annals of history are replete with persecution practiced in the name of religion. Those pages which pertain to the inquisition are chronicles of the most refined and inexorable cruelty. Particulars include the massacre of Protestants by Catholics, and of Protestant retaliation. Jews have been persecuted throughout history. They have been discriminated against, exploited, robbed and slaughtered without redress, for there were no laws to protect them.

Religion, when in power, has everywhere shown intolerance toward other religions. John Calvin, a fugitive from the Sorbonne's theological tyrants, went on to establish his own reign of terror in Geneva, which till then had enjoyed a reputation for religious tolerance. Calvin caused the physician Servetus to be burned alive because he had attacked the dogma of the Holy Trinity and denied the divinity of Jesus. Called upon for the last time to repudiate his blasphemy, Servetus answered, "I cannot deny what my reason has allowed me to understand. All things are part of God, all creatures are part of his essence."[8] He was condemned by the Catholics, who burned him in effigy, and also by the Protestants, who burned him in the flesh. A generation later, Giordano Bruno would express essentially the same idea and would also go to the stake.

Jews have never been in a position to inflict this kind of punishment upon dissenters. In Holland, however, where they were enjoying protection from Spanish persecution, they themselves showed intolerance toward a coreligionist who had reneged on their teachings. They excommunicated Baruch Spinoza on July 27, 1656. Subsequently, he lived outside the church, and his writings became a source of inspiration to people like Goethe, Lessing, Shelley, and many others.

Voltaire, the eighteenth century's most renowned French philosopher, devoted much time and talent to combating religious intolerance. One case in which he became involved had repercussions throughout Europe. It had to do with a man named Callas, who was falsely accused of having killed his son, in order to prevent his renouncing the Protestant faith to become a Catholic. The man was tortured and burned at the stake. Voltaire undertook to prove his innocence, using his own money and connections and sparing no effort. In 1765 he was successful in clearing Callas's name and restoring his good repute. It was after this affair that Voltaire wrote his *Treatise on Intolerance.*

The Fear of Hell: A Means of Domination

Christianity has instilled in its followers the fear of hell as a way of maintaining its dominance in their lives. Throughout the Middle Ages, right up until the Renaissance, this threat of damnation hovered over Christians, and only total submission to the dictates of the Church could bring relief. The Church claimed to be the instrument of God's will and the arbiter of man's fate. Using excommunication as its weapon, the Church became more powerful than the state; even emperors were subject to its authority, a fact illustrated by the well-known event which took place at a castle called Canossa. It was in the courtyard of this castle that Henry IV waited to see Pope Gregory. For three days the Emperor stood there barefoot and bareheaded (Jan. 25–28, 1077). Finally, he was admitted and the Pope removed the ban of excommunication. Not just individuals, but entire communities, cities, and even a whole country could be struck down by this awful weapon. An excommunicated person could not attend Mass or receive the holy sacraments. To be deprived of these was considered, in the somber atmosphere of that time, as tantamount to damnation. But this was not all; he was an outcast from the community and even his friends turned away in fear. When a town came under the interdict, it was deprived of all religious services; there was no ringing of bells, no religious burials, and no baptisms; no confessions nor absolutions. When churches were closed to them in this way, people felt condemned by God.

Dante's *Inferno* amply demonstrates how powerfully this concept of hell and damnation acted upon the human mind. The first part of his trilogy, *The Divine Comedy,* is a compendium of sadistic justice; each sin is categorized along with the punishment which automatically applies to it. There is no forgiveness for the damned, since all punishment is for eternity. The door of Hell bears the following inscription:

> "Through me the way is to the City of Woe.
> Through me the way into eternal pain . . .
> Relinquish all hope, ye who enter here."[9]

16

A mere enumeration of the tortures inflicted on sinners "by supreme wisdom and primal love," as the poet conceives it, will illustrate the Christian mentality of the early fourteenth century. Those guilty of carnal sins are blown about forever on stormy winds; the gluttonous are showered with icy rain; misers and spendthrifts roll dead weights from opposite directions, and when they collide, rail at each other. Heretics must dwell forever in flaming sepulchres; those guilty of violent assault are doomed to a boiling river of blood. Suicides have become withered, poisonous trees among which Harpies cry; those who have cursed God must lie in burning sand forever; usurers sit huddled up; those who have violated nature, by which Dante means people we would now call "gay," move continually in a fiery rain; those buying or selling church offices are fixed head downward in rock; the faces of sorcerers and diviners are twisted so they must look behind them; those trafficking in public office are submerged in boiling pitch and kept under by demons with long hooks; hypocrites are pacing in copes of lead; thieves are tormented by serpents; they burn to ashes but the ashes immediately resume their former shape, so the torments begin all over again; evil counselors are imprisoned in burning flames; those who caused a schism in the official religion are horribly mutilated; forgers are afflicted with loathsome diseases and lie helpless and inert; a frozen lake contains those who have betrayed their country. Those who betrayed hospitality and killed their guests are imprisoned in ice along with Lucifer.

The poet Dante was one of the most eloquent and articulate exponents of medieval beliefs. His description of Hell was a vivid summary of the horrors conjured up by the priests in their pulpits in order to frighten people. The early Teutons called Hell the place under the earth to which everyone, good or bad, went after death. The Old Testament uses the word "Sheol," which signifies much the same thing, an abode under the earth for the departed. In Sheol there were no moral distinctions either, no reward for virtue nor punishment for crime.

17

Greeks and Romans also believed in an underworld for the dead, but here their behavior in life was weighed and judged accordingly. Buddhism has no less than 136 hells, with a gradation in the intensity of pain commensurate with the sins committed in life. Christianity, however, was the only religion which used hell as a weapon with which to threaten people, to terrify them in order to obtain obedience.

It might be supposed that in this enlightened era, the threat of hell could no longer frighten anyone, but such is not the case. Preachers still brandish this weapon before the gullible. The *Los Angeles Times* ran a story on January 16, 1984 about a pastor named Billy Dean in Swansea, North Carolina. Pacing the main street of this small town, the pastor is said to have shouted, "God's wrath has waxed hot on Swansea!" A handful of his Bible students, well-scrubbed and earnest, had gathered nearby and exclaimed fervently, "Amen, brother!"

The pastor obviously used this threat of damnation, which has proved so effective down the centuries, to get attention and increase his audience. But the townspeople found him a nuisance because his preaching kept buyers away from the stores. So they had the city council issue an ordinance which prohibited preaching on the street without a permit. Whereupon an association of preachers decided to sue the town, claiming that the ordinance violated the free speech guaranteed by the Constitution.

Nor is this an isolated case. Heaven and hell have remained the preacher's stock in trade. The substance of their message can be reduced to these two words, "Jesus" and "damnation." The first constitutes the attraction, the second the menace, by means of which they hold their audiences. Enlightened men would like to banish hell from this earth, not just the physical misery, but the hell which exists in men's minds. But this is no easy task. They are up against those who have a vested interest in keeping it aflame both here and in the hereafter.

Religion Is Anthropocentric

Man does not seem to realize that his life on earth is very precarious. He is convinced that everything which exists on

18

this planet, including all other creatures, has been created for his benefit. Could he ever concede that every living thing, whether it be a snail or a swallow, a fish or a lion, is as much part of the great plan of creation, as important or as unimportant as man himself? And they rarely, if ever, give a thought to the cosmos, of which our earth and the solar system and the galaxy in which it is located are but an infinitely small parcel of the universe. They imagine man to be the center of the universe, just as their predecessors imagined the earth to be the center around which the sun revolved—until Copernicus set things right. Swollen with the pride of human greatness, they believe that God himself must bow before man and do his bidding. Unless they chasten their thoughts, unless they cease to think of the Creator as having a human shape, a benevolent uncle, heeding their not always quite clean requests, man will not be able to transcend himself, for God is what a man makes him to be. What man needs is not a manlike God, but a Godlike man. Indeed, unless man transcends himself, he will destroy himself. Evolution is imperative, especially in the realm of the spirit. The true mission of man is to become greater than himself. If he does not live up to his mission he will be replaced; such is the law of evolution.

Religion Fosters Superstition, Fraud, Exploitation of Simple Minds Aspiring to Reach Up to God

There is a particularly ugly and dangerous aspect of religion, namely, that it lends itself to the exploitation of simple minds, of people who aspire to rise above the misery of their daily lives, ennoble themselves by elevating their thoughts to God. They turn to the church to help them in this endeavor. The preacher is in their eyes a holy man, intermediary between them and God. His words are sanctified through his communication with the highest, so they must be believed implicitly. Unfortunately, there have always been, and there are today, many contemptible individuals who exploit this simple faith and play upon the veneration they inspire, in order to enrich themselves.

In earlier times, the papacy itself had set a bad example with such practices. Ecclesiastic offices had to be bought. In addition to this, the Roman curia issued letters of indulgence, by which, it was said, souls languishing in Purgatory could be pardoned and admitted to Paradise. The sale of these letters was assigned to agents who received a commission on these transactions. The whole scheme was a colossal fraud, aimed at extracting huge sums from the working classes, sums pocketed by the Pope.

Martin Luther, a German monk and teacher of theology at the University of Wittenberg, was incensed about this shameful exploitation of popular gullibility. He affixed 95 theses to the door of the cathedral in Wittenberg, inviting debates, which was a customary practice at the time. "How can the Pope pardon sins without repentance?" was the question he raised.

This document was the match which set aflame the whole Christian world of that day.

This exploitation of the poor and simple-minded by unscrupulous preachers is as prevalent today as it was in the Middle Ages. Western democracies offer especially great opportunities for such fraud because in these countries religion is protected by law. Churches enjoy special privileges which glib talkers, "the merchants of God," are quick to make use of. Anyone can found a new religion and attract attention by the use of flamboyant oratory punctuated by dramatic gestures. Shouting is effective, along with music which arouses religious fervor. There are exhortations to repent, to come forward and be saved. The audience is urged to respond with loud "Amens" and applause, the object being to arouse a sort of religious ecstasy, or mass euphoria.

Some of these religious hucksters accumulate a scandalous amount of money. If they possess charisma, they can exert a kind of hypnotic power over their audiences. It follows that the faithful can often be induced to donate everything that they own to the religious organization. It was reported that one of these demagogues, an immigrant from India, owns some sixty

20

thousand acres of land which he surveys daily, riding around in one of his many Mercedes cars. He claims that he is God, that he has taken mortal form in order to descend from Heaven and visit mankind. Another has a large portrait of himself attached to the wall of the television studio where he appears. This portrait shows him with arms raised heavenward, and he is surrounded by psychedelic pictures. He claims that, inspired by God, he lapses into strange tongues and the camera is focused on him as he mouths this mumbo-jumbo of disjointed phrases, punctuated by grunts and gestures. He says he was born a Russian Jew and saw the light at age 14, when he learned of Jesus Christ.

Still other preachers claim to have healing powers. One of these spoke to a woman, obviously an accomplice, who had come forward in a wheelchair posing as a cripple. He placed his hand upon her head and ordered her to walk, which she did, while the faithful applauded. Some preachers claim the gift of prophesy; in fact, there is no end to the artifice used by these religious con men who proliferate because of the public's incredible naivete. The most shocking example of what power one of these fanatics can wield is the tragedy in Guiana. A black man named Jones was pastor of an American church called the "People's Temple." He persuaded a number of the members, both families and single persons, to leave their homes and follow him to Guiana, South America, where they established a colony. Here, Jones could do as he liked with his people, the place being so remote from the watchful eye of the law. The brothers were to till the land and the sisters to do the household chores; the prettiest of the women were privileged to give the holy man a good time in bed.

The American Congress got wind of irregularities in the management of the colony and sent out representatives to investigate them. Jones had one of these Congressmen assassinated. Fearing the consequences of his action, he decided to commit suicide and, to demonstrate the frightful power which a demented preacher can exercise over feeble minds, he prevailed upon his flock to join him! Every one of them, men, women and children, drank poison and died with him, their bodies left to rot in the tropical sun.

The exploitation of religious faith can take many forms. During the Middle Ages, the sale of so-called relics of saints was a flourishing trade. Some temples, as well as other particular locales, were said to contain the bones of saints. And there was an endless variety of other "sacred" items offered, such as hair supposed to have come from the head of Jesus. All of this goes to prove that, historically, human gullibility has had no limits.

Today's preachers, drunk with power, have raised their sights. They aim at influencing politics in those countries whose protection they enjoy. They thunder against humanists and liberals, whom they equate with communists. They say that voting, for them, is a sin against God. They move to small towns in such numbers that eventually they constitute the majority. Then they can take over the city council and enact ordinances which favor their interests. All of this represents a great danger to democratic institutions. Clearly, the intention of these emboldened religionists, whatever their persuasion, is focused upon seizing powers of state. Then they could establish a regime similar to the one in Islam, namely, a sort of fundamentalist republic which would ban freedom of thought and exact conformity to religious tenets. Today, these latter-day Knights of Torquemata are burning books, tomorrow, should they have the power, they would burn people. Then darkness would descend upon the human mind.

This encroaching fundamentalism seems a paradox in our technological world; nevertheless, the menace exists and is not to be taken lightly. Periods of great progress in human thinking often coincide with movements that are extremely reactionary. The defeat of democracy often results in cruel and cynical dictatorship; recent history in Chile and Argentina illustrates this truth.

Witch-Hunts

The belief in witchcraft was a type of superstition which victimized mostly women. They were accused of consorting with the devil in order to cast evil spells. These were supposed to bring every sort of misfortune, from turning cow's milk sour to causing illness or even death. These irrational beliefs were responsible for the torture and death of many innocent women.

In the 13th century, an enlightened king, Coloman of Hungary, declared, "Witches do not exist"; nevertheless, the belief in them has persisted up to this very day. The Inquisition called the practice of witchcraft a heresy and punished it as such. The Old Testament declares in Exodus, 22:18: "Thou shalt not suffer a witch to live." In 1485 a book called *The Witches' Hammer* was published. It was the work of a fanatic and had disastrous consequences. In France, thousands of women were put to death; one judge in Nancy is reported to have condemned 800 culprits in six years; in Toulouse, 600 women perished at a single execution, and at Treves 7,000 were burnt or drowned. It is said, however, that the witch trials in Scotland were even more terrible.

Leaders of the Reformation, far from putting a stop to these horrors, encouraged them. Luther, Calvin, and Wesley were all advocates. Panic had spread to the United States and came to a head in 1692 with the famous witch trial at Salem, Massachusetts. It had been preceded by a sort of mass hysteria among certain young women, who were taken with convulsions during which they seemed to be choking, and who spoke in strange voices. Some of them screamed that they were being strangled by a black shadow. These phenomena often took place in church during public prayer. Parents of the victims consulted physicians, who declared that the girls were possessed by demons. This affliction spread among the villagers, until it became epidemic. Fear and suspicion gripped all hearts—fear that witches were among them, ready to corrupt and destroy. Anyone might be a witch, but elderly women were especially mistrusted. A number of suspects were arrested and subjected to torture. Some confessed to being in communication with the devil. In all, sixteen women were hanged.

This is not to say that the residents of Salem were any more superstitious than the general population of the United States at that time. The hanging of these innocent women was due, in part, to the ignorance and fear which these early settlers thought they had left behind them in the old country. But there were other causes. Sometimes these trials were prompted, as they were during the Inquisition, by the desire to satisfy a personal grudge or to appropriate the accused person's property.

Exorcism

The belief in witches is correlated to the belief that evil spirits will, for some reason, inhabit the body of a person, make it speak in changed voices, commit violence or other uncommon acts, "possess" a person. Demonology is a science invented and elaborated by priests. To deliver a possessed person from the evil spirit, a complete ritual has been worked out. Priests must learn to what procedures they must resort, what prayers to recite. Psychology and psychiatry have occupied themselves with such phenomena, classifying them as hysterical, schizoid, or paranoid. The conditions which science cannot account for as yet, such as possessions, remain a still unconquered domain of psychiatry which will be conquered some day, just as cancer will. There is no need to attribute such phenomena to the devil, unless one ascribes all crimes committed in obedience to voices, to the command of a second ego, to hallucinations, the many aspects of incomprehensible crimes, to the work of the devil.

Mental disorders frequently manifest themselves in strange forms. The power of the mind over matter is a largely unexplored domain; it might be terrific, unsuspected at the present time. Discoveries in this domain might yield fantastic results, open a new chapter in psychology. The brain is the new frontier in medical science. Science still proves powerless in certain cases, and religion steps in wherever there is a vacuum to fill. The sufferers look for help wherever they hope to find it.

To call the priest in order to deliver a person from demons is not different from calling a Christian Science healer to pray

24

over a sick child. The child might even recover, the possessed person might even be delivered from demons, not because, but in spite or regardless of the incantations on his behalf.

Religion Fosters Hypocrisy

The observance of religious rites is often taken for true piety. Yet it may cover carnal passions and evil designs. The 17th century French playwright, Molière, immortalized this type of religious hypocrisy in "Tartuffe." The protagonist poses as the most pious of men, and has made such an impression on his host that this poor deluded man has given him all he owns. Tartuffe is finally unmasked when he attempts to seduce his benefactor's wife, after which he orders the man out of the house which he no longer owns. Stendhal, writing in the 19th century, has also dealt with the theme of religious hypocrisy in his famous novel, *The Black and the Red*. It tells the story of a brilliant young man living in the post-Napoleonic era, who finds that because he is poor, the church is his only means of getting ahead in life. Being ambitious, he feels compelled to feign the religious devotion required for the priesthood.

The Roman Catholic religion forbids divorce because it holds that marriages are made in heaven and therefore it is sinful to dissolve them. Yet everyone knows that throughout history, and even in our own day, marriages have been arranged for material, social, or political advantage. Marriage between royal families was an instrument of foreign policy. The ban on divorce forced ordinary couples to stay together when they no longer felt any affection, perhaps even hated one another. Like galley slaves, they were chained to each other for life. The upper classes consoled themselves by finding partners outside of matrimony. This custom was considered perfectly normal. The more influential, if they were determined, could always manage to get an annulment. Henry VIII of England was a notorious exception. He wanted to divorce Catherine of Aragon so that he could marry Anne Boleyn. The clergy who argued his case maintained that Catherine had first been betrothed to the King's brother, and although he died before they could marry, the vow she had made was still binding. This meant that her marriage to Henry was invalid. The Pope refused to accept this argument because Catherine was a Spanish princess and Spain had very close ties to Rome. So the annulment was not granted, and as a result, England broke all ties with the Roman Church. The King was then declared Supreme Head of the Church of England. This decision had grave consequences later on.

In Italy, marriage was held to be indissoluble until recent times; now Italian law permits civil divorce.

Religion Rests on Faith

Religion tolerates no inquiry and furnishes no proof. "You must believe" is the stereotypical answer given to a would-be convert who wishes to inquire about the source of some legend or Biblical story. The surrender of reason is a requirement for joining any organized religion. Dogma is not subject to proof.

The Bible, which is the Christians' Holy Book, is said to have been inspired by God, even though it is clear that many of the stories it contains originated in ancient legend and folklore. Moses is supposed to have gone up on Mount Sinai, where God presented him with the Ten Commandments written on tablets of stone. Muhammad climbed another mountain where he was given the Koran, which is the Muslims' Holy Book. It is said that this book is not only inspired by God but contains His own words. As for the Mormons, we are asked to believe that the angel Moroni came down to earth and presented a tablet to their prophet, Joseph Smith. The message was written in a strange tongue which the angel helped him to translate.

Another dogma of the Christian Church is the belief of the immaculate conception, or the divinity of The Christ. The "credo quia absurdum" (I believe *because* it is absurd) is a motto often encountered in religious writings. The *because* is puzzling. You would think that these mystics would say, "I believe it in spite of its being absurd." To them, it would seem that the dogma's absurdity is the very thing which makes it believable. Such belief, however, cannot be had on demand, and reason does not easily surrender to the absurd.

Religion Is Authoritarian

The major religions claim that their tenets are based on revelation and are therefore inalterable. The Roman Catholic Pope claims infallibility in all his pronouncements. The Greek church also made this claim for the decrees handed down by its council, which it looked upon as ecumenical.

The Roman Church bases its claim of infallibility upon the Gospel according to St. Matthew, 28:19, which says: "Go ye therefore and teach all nations," and Mark 16:15, which says: "Go ye into all the world and teach the gospel to every creature." By virtue of the Gospels, the Church can never receive or embrace any erroneous doctrine, but must perpetually teach only these basic truths of God. In 1870, the Vatican Council decreed that when the Roman Pontiff speaks *ex cathedra*, that is, in his role of Pastor and Doctor to all Christians, whatever ruling he lays down is binding for the Universal Church. The position taken by the Church on any question concerning faith and morals is defined by the Vicar of Christ. His rulings are believed to be divinely inspired and therefore unchangeable.

When the infallibility of the Pope was first proclaimed by the Vatican Council, it stirred up a lot of controversy and still does to this day. It is, in fact, one of the main obstacles to any reunion of Catholics and Protestants since the split caused by the Reformation.

The very name, *Catholic*, which in Greek and Latin means "universal," shows plainly that Christianity lays claim to being the only true religion, its truth embracing all mankind. Thus, according to Christian belief, those who have not been baptized may not enter Paradise. In Dante's *Divine Comedy*, the sages and poets of antiquity must dwell in Limbo. Virgil cannot lead Dante all the way; he is replaced by Dante's childhood love, Beatrice, at the gate to Paradise. Mormons are now baptizing, post mortem, the ancestors of their church members.

27

Religions other than Christianity are also authoritarian. The original meaning of the Jewish *Torah* is "oracle" and anyone who attempted a critical study of the Koran in any Islamic republic would be placing his life in jeopardy.

Religious authoritarianism and religion mixing with politics manifest themselves today as in the past, albeit in different ways. During the presidential campaign of Ronald Reagan in 1984 abortion was a political issue. Roman Catholic bishops on the East Coast of the United States attacked two prominent lay persons for suggesting that there was some latitude in the teaching of abortion. A statement to the same effect was signed by 97 other Catholic notables and was published in New York. It asserted that the authentic Catholic position was not as absolutely restrictive as the bishops in question had indicated.

In 1984, a week before Christmas the news broke that the Vatican (technically the Sacred Congregation of Religious and Secular Institutes) had contacted the superiors of the 24 women and demanded that these women retract their statement or be dismissed from their religious communities. In effect these women, whose vulnerability comes from their lifetime choice to serve in the Church, were asked to admit that they were ignorant or dishonest in signing the statement, or to say dishonestly that they were wrong and had since changed their minds. The attitude of the Catholic Church has not changed since Galilei Galileo: it seeks fidelity rather than the truth; its authority is rooted in power than in truth.

Religious Fanaticism Blunts the Mind and Endangers People's Health

Religious fanatics have an otherwordly attitude toward life. They do not keep pace with progress. A Christian Scientist, if he falls ill, and if he follows the unadulterated teaching of his church, will not resort to medical science, but will call a practitioner who will pray for him. This he hopes will cure his bleeding ulcer or his kidney troubles. The congregation that calls itself Jehovah's Witnesses or the "Watchtower" would

28

rather let their sick children die than send for a doctor or allow them to be taken to a hospital. Often, authorities must intervene and take children from their parents for treatment. One must despair of such backwardness, narrow-mindedness and cruelty.

Then there are those who keep their children out of public schools to protect them from contamination with worldly ideas. These children are taught by uncertified teachers who instill in them the narrow viewpoint and prejudices of their parents. These children will be at a disadvantage when they go to higher schools and mingle with others of their own age. Their education will prove to be full of gaps and thus lacking cohesion, as well as narrow in scope. They will be unaccustomed to logical or scientific reasoning.

Orthodox Jews expose their children to still another kind of danger. Israeli children are, as a rule, physically beautiful and well developed; they also seem happy and self-confident. The children of Orthodox Jews, or Hassidim, are an exception. It suffices to watch them coming out of school, to notice that those of orthodox parents tend to be puny and weak-looking. This is because they spend twice as many hours studying, for in addition to public school, they must also attend Jewish religious school. This leaves them very little time to play in the open air. Their minds are overloaded and their physical development is stunted.

Religion Is Often Mixed with Politics

Religious pretexts are often used to achieve political aims, and vice-versa. Ever since the foundation of the Holy Roman Empire, beginning in the year 800, when the Pope crowned Charlemagne, the Church has been closely associated with the Crown. For a thousand years, the spiritual power of the Church was supported by the worldly power of the Emperor. The Pope appointed Church dignitaries, but the Emperor had to confirm them. Church and Crown were interdependent.

The Thirty Years' War, which devastated the European continent, was begun in the name of religion. Actually, it was a struggle for territory and, in the end, religious reasons for the fight were all but forgotten. In France, Catholics massacred Protestants, and Protestants murdered Catholics in the naked pursuit of power.

Today, Catholics and Protestants are once more at war in Northern Ireland. This time the conflict has no religious motivation. This bloody battle is being waged by the Irish Republican Army in an attempt to force the British to give up their sovereignty. Northern Ireland could then be attached to Ireland proper. Catholics there feel like second class citizens because Protestants control the economic life of the country. This situation has come about because of the higher birth rate among Catholics, which is due to the fact that the Church forbids birth control. Too many children means poverty and lack of education, a vicious circle from which Catholics cannot escape. The same situation prevails in Canada. There, English speaking people, the majority of whom are Protestants, dominate business, education, and politics. This has caused discontent among French Catholics and the same feeling of inferiority that we find in the Irish. As a result, there is now a political party in French-speaking Quebec which advocates secession from Canada.

Recent events in Iran are a striking example of religion being mixed with politics. In 1978, the Shah was overthrown by the joint efforts of the clergy and Western-oriented civilians. Once the revolution had been accomplished, the clergy acquired political power and eliminated its former allies. The mullahs established a reign of terror, abolishing all democratic institutions in an effort to stamp out Western influence. Women were relegated to the inferior role imposed by the Koran—that of total subjection to male dominance. Iran was then attacked by Iraq, a neighboring Arab country, which attempted to seize some disputed territory. Iran countered this attack with ferocity. At this writing the battle has been going on for five years, growing ever more violent. Countless thousands have died, males of all ages, some of them only children. One news photographer brought back a picture showing corpses four feet deep along the passage to a road which Iranians were trying to occupy because it leads to Basra, Iraq's only seaport. The war has been prolonged by the will of the Ayatolla Komeini, Iran's religious leader, who has vowed to establish in Iraq the same kind of Shia Muslim regime which he has instituted at home. It has already been pointed out that Muslim soldiers do not fear death, being convinced that if they fall in battle they will wake up in Paradise, a fact which adds greatly to the ferocity of this war.

In Lebanon we find the same struggle for power wearing a religious guise. But here it is more complex; Muslim fights Muslim, and a sect that calls itself Druze fights both Muslims and Christians, though occasionally it joins one of them against the other. In addition, splinter groups under various names fight against each other, and also against Israel, which they consider the arch enemy.

If this power struggle were ever settled in favor of the Muslims, they would establish the same kind of religious dictatorship that now prevails in Iran. In fact, Islam is not only politically oriented, but conquest by war is an inherent feature of this religion.

In the United States there has been a resurgence of attempts to introduce religion into national institutions. Of course, Americans call themselves a nation under God, their coins bear the words "In God We Trust," but they are also inscribed with the word "Liberty," and the Constitution stipulates the separation of church and state. There are those with strong religious feelings, like our current President, who would like school children to begin the day with a prayer. The majority of the population, however, oppose this idea, and rightly so, because once religion is introduced into public schools, there is danger that young minds will be indoctrinated by whatever religion predominates in the particular area. What seems to be a small step to begin with, could in the end undermine the secular character of the country, which is the very essence of a democracy. It is to be hoped that the present generation has learned from the past to be wary. Religious freedom is inseparable from political freedom, and the price of freedom, as we know, is eternal vigilance.

Religion Versus Science

Most religionists are at odds with scientific thinking and investigation. People who need to examine and analyze make them uncomfortable. These scientists question their simplistic teachings about the origin of life and man's place in the universe.

The most serious objection one can make to religion is that it does not evolve. Preachers claim to have received the truth from God, that He has spoken to them. They believe this truth to be final and not subject to change or amendment, just as the Pope's pronouncements are supposed to be unalterable. Yet, as man advances in knowledge, his view of the universe, of the creator and creation necessarily change. Religious leaders fear the conflict between their final truth and the findings of modern science. Science tells us that man can never completely solve the mystery of the universe because he himself is part of the universe. Science is humble; it can only hope that step by step, it will unravel a little more of the mystery. With awe and reverence the scientist faces the unresolved questions which each new discovery brings to the surface. These enigmas challenge the human mind: and that mind itself is something to marvel at, and to be cherished, for it is his ability to reason which makes man what he is: a Searcher and unique upon this planet.

Chapter II

REFLECTIONS ON THE BOOK OF GENESIS

The Book of Genesis can be divided into two parts: the story of the creation proper, which concludes with the expulsion of Adam and Eve from Paradise, and the story of the multiplication of mankind—which is really the story of the origin of the Jewish people.

Genesis begins with this statement: "In the beginning God created the heaven and the earth."

In the beginning. Was there ever a beginning to the infinity of time? If there had been, then there would also be an end, and when time stopped, the universe would vanish with it. Presumably, it would dissolve into nothingness, but nothingness is a concept that is quite unimaginable in reference to the universe. Even if our planet and our galaxy should disappear, even though the universe exploded with a new big bang, something would always remain, because nothingness simply isn't conceivable.

What did God do before He created heaven and earth? The author(s) of Genesis obviously considered our earth to be the center of the universe, because subsequently we read that He made the stars in order to illuminate the earth. So it would seem that the stars were created after the earth was finished.

Again we ask: What was God doing before the creation? Did he just hover over the original Chaos? And who created Chaos? Because it, too, had to arise from something. Can we imagine God without any universe, existing for aeons in the void, before he decided to create heaven and earth?

Genesis 1:3: And God said, "Let there be light and there was light." This, before the creation of the sun. Was there light before the creation of the sun? We know that our planet does

33

not have its own light. Did God remove it after He had created the sun and stars?

Genesis 1:4: "And God saw the light, that it was good." Here is the beginning of an anthropomorphic conception of the Creator which debases Him, though the intent was to extoll Him. Didn't God know, being omniscient, that the light would be good? Could He be satisfied that it was so, only after the experiment had succeeded? Those who wrote the Book present God as being like a scientist at work in his laboratory.

Further on in Genesis 1:4: "God divided the light from darkness." God held the darkness in one hand, and in the other he held light. The light and the darkness were alternated, and this was day and night. But we know that while one side of the earth is light, the other half is dark, that night and day always exist simultaneously. The authors of The Book were not aware of this. At least there is no mention made of it.

Genesis 1:20: And God said, "Let the waters bring forth abundantly the moving creature that hath life, and fowl that may fly above the earth in the open firmament of heaven." This verse and verses 21 and 22 echo the teaching of the early Greek philosopher Thales, who lived around 700 B.C., long before the Book of Genesis was written. He taught that the original principle of all things is water, from which everything has come forth. This is the so-called Neptunist theory, which has survived up to the present time. In the 18th century its foremost exponent was the German scientist Abraham Gottlob Werner. He maintained that all land creatures, including man, have preserved in their bodies some organs, now degenerated, which are remainders of their erstwhile existence in water. His views were espoused by the German scientist-poet Johann Wolfgang von Goethe. In the latter's major work, *Faust*, Proteus advises Homunculus, the spirit conjured up by man, desirous of being born: "On the broad ocean's breast must thou begin!"

It is interesting to note that in Werner's and Goethe's time there was heated controversy between creationists and evolutionists, just as there is today, though in a somewhat different form. In those days the evolutionists were known as Neptunists, and their opposites were the plutonists, who held that creation could occur suddenly with no previous evolutionary process, as in the mutations of species. Such occurrences would contradict the long process of development that the Neptunists felt was evident everywhere in the universe.

Genesis 1:26 offers the statement, attributed to God, that man was made in His own image, "after our likeness." This corroborates the anthropomorphic concept of God. How is this to be understood? Does God have a body, such as we have? Is he male or female, or is he hermaphroditic?

Genesis 1:27: "Male and female created he them." This refers to the human race, because 1:28 adds: And God blessed them, and God said unto them, "Be fruitful and multiply, and replenish the earth, and subdue it: and have dominion over the fish of the sea, and over the fowl of the air, and over every living thing that moveth upon the earth." This section is in direct contradiction to the subsequent statement 2:5, "And there was not a man to till the ground," as well as to the following one, 2:7, "And the Lord God formed man of the dust of the ground, and breathed into his nostrils the breath of life; and man became a living soul," after which begins the tale about the Garden of Eden. It seems apparent that the contradictory parts just cited were not written by the same author as Genesis 1:27. Also, one is uncomfortable with the words "replenish the earth," though this may come from a flaw in the translation from the original texts. Indeed, the verb "replenish" suggests that at one time there was a plenitude of human beings.

The Book of Genesis is explicit about man's dominion over all other creatures of the planet; in fact, it expresses the belief that all creatures exist only to ensure man's survival and comfort. The Book not only makes man in the image of God, it also makes him the center of the creation. This anthropocentric presentation of the creation has survived to this very day.

Reflection tells us, however, that human beings are just as ephemeral as dinosaurs were, and that one day they will be replaced by other creatures, better adapted to the environment then prevailing on the planet. Already we are fighting a never-ending battle with the insects, and every day it becomes harder to win this fight.

Genesis 2:2: "God rested on the seventh day from all the work he had made." Once more that anthropomorphic image of God. Did he, as would an ordinary mortal, need to rest from his work? Was he tired? Yet, this passage of the Book is useful, as a model and a warning to remember. If God himself had to rest one day a week, human beings surely need this, too. The setting aside of one day out of seven in order to collect and reflect on oneself, to be more than just a beast of burden—the idea of the Sabbath—a day to enjoy life, originated with the Jews. They were the ones who first practiced this custom after they had been deported to the Roman Empire. The philosopher Seneca was dubious about it, and said that this was the cause of his aversion to the Jewish people. The writer(s) of this passage most likely attributed to the Creator what his (or their) people had long adopted in their daily lives.

Genesis 2:9: "God planted the tree of life in the Garden of Eden and also the tree of knowledge of good and evil."

Why did God plant these trees in the Garden where he placed the first man? Did he plan the scenario which followed, the temptation of Eve by the serpent and the fact that both she and Adam would succumb to it, eating of the forbidden fruit? The knowledge of good and evil is obviously an awareness of sex and of the fact that they could enjoy it with each other. The evil here is the enjoyment of sexual pleasure by man and woman.

Genesis 2:17 refers to the forbidden fruit. One thing is forbidden, while all others are permitted to him. This is a motif which we find in many folktales. It is best illustrated in the story of Bluebeard, who told his wife that she could enter any room in the castle but one. To go in there would be fatal. In

36

the same section of Genesis, there is also reference to this penalty of death: "For in the day that thou eatest thereof, thou shalt surely die." Though this threat is never carried out, it seems likely that the idea was, indeed, borrowed from folk tales, and inserted into the Book of Genesis.

Genesis 2:19–25: God creates the woman from man's rib. Why a woman? Why not another man for a companion? The underlying idea is that the woman must complement, or rather, complete man in the Great Design of the Creator. "They [man and woman] shall be one flesh," says Genesis 2:24, but, at this juncture, they are still innocent, they don't know how this could be accomplished. Genesis 2:25: "They were naked, the man and his wife, and they were not ashamed."

Genesis 3 relates the story of the original sin. The serpent becomes the symbol of cunning, of evil, of a rebel to the Great Design. If this is so, why did God create it? Did he intend it to lead man astray? Could the serpent have told Adam and Eve the great secret, namely, that they were sexual creatures and could enjoy each other, unless God had first created them in such a way that they should be "one flesh" by the act of sexual intercourse? The bodily particularities of both the man and the woman definitely served God's plan, which was the multiplication of the human race. If so, why was it wrong? The whole story of the original sin is absurd. Yet, figuratively, it has great significance. Man, having chosen this woman, emancipates himself from parental tutelage; he is henceforth on his own. But the Book of Genesis presents this as punishment, not as the natural development of life.

Presenting the satisfaction of the flesh as a sin served the purpose of the Church. Many young people developed a guilt complex because of this thesis, that was inculcated in them. The Church wanted this to happen, so as to exercise its sway over the souls.

The warning "in the day thou eatest thereof thou shalt surely die" is incomprehensible in the context. Indeed, Adam and Eve were as ignorant of the meaning of death as is a child; they

37

were children in their innocence. And, as we said before, the threat was not carried out, which leaves God in the position of a parent who threatens but does not think of executing his threat. God is weak, vacillating, a poor educator.

Did God not foresee what would happen between the first man and woman? Or was it his intention to maintain these in an innocent state, thus assuring that these first humans would have no offspring, the only carriers of God's image? Or did he plan to create more humans from the dust of the earth? Is it not more logical to assume that he wanted man to multiply by his own means rather than doing this job for him? Surely, one can say: if one takes this story of the original sin seriously, then God was either confused or he did not play a straight game!

Genesis 3:14: God cursed the serpent and said: "After the fall, upon thy belly shalt thou go, and dust shalt thou eat all the days of thy life." This again shows complete ignorance of natural history. The serpent eats anything but dust. Its life would be exempt from the struggle for survival if it could satisfy its hunger with dust, for dust is abundant everywhere. It goes upon its belly, but this is how it was created, and is as natural to it as flying is to the bird. This tale reveals a naive narrator who speaks to a naive audience.

Genesis 3:15: Refers to the pain of childbirth and then adds: "thy desire shall be to thy husband, and he shall rule over thee." This passage shows that woman was regarded as subordinate to man, a concept which prevailed in both Eastern and Western societies, and which has begun to break down only in our own day. Man attributes his own ideas to God and thus makes God into a male chauvinist.

Genesis 3:22: And the Lord God said, "Behold, the man is become as one of us." The language is incomprehensible. Why the word "us"? It is not a simple *pluralis majestatis,* for if it were that, it would not be preceded by the word "one." It would say "become like us." "One of us" connotes several gods or a multiplicity of spirits. God drove Adam out of the Garden of

Eden, lest he eat from the fruit of the tree of life and live forever. If that happened, man would be a god himself. And God could not tolerate that, though he created man in his own image.

The story (proper) of creation, as it has been analyzed above, constitutes the prelude to the story of the Jewish people. In this second part of Genesis, several episodes stand out.

THE STORY OF CAIN AND ABEL

First, the killing of Abel by his brother, Cain. The cause for this first fratricide was, according to Genesis 4:4 and 4:5, "the Lord had respect for Abel's offering and had no respect for Cain's." In other words, God discriminated between the brothers, favoring Abel over Cain. He was therefore the cause of Cain's jealousy and must share the responsibility for Cain's slaying of his brother. At least this would be the impartial ruling of a judge if the case had involved ordinary mortals.

What is the purpose of telling us this Cain-Abel episode, the first in the endless chronicle of murders of humans by fellow humans? Obviously, by the time Genesis was written, such murders had become commonplace, and to be complete, human history must include this aspect of human nature.

The mark of Cain is a most ingenious symbol. It represents the guilty conscience which accompanies the murderer everywhere, and gives him no peace. He imagines that all can see his hideous deed. It is the blood that Macbeth cannot wash off his hands. It excludes him from the human race.

Genesis 4:16: "And Cain went out from the presence of the Lord, and dwelt in the land of Nod, on the east of Eden." There is no end of inconsistencies in the text. Here again, the Lord is portrayed as a human father that one can hide from. This seems a debasing image to anyone conceiving of God as a sublime, august spirit. And to say that Cain dwelt in the land of Nod implies that Nod already existed, although there had been no reference to it previously.

And the next paragraph, "And Cain knew his wife" is amazing. As Clarence Darrow asked at the Salem trial: "Who was she? Where did she meet him?" The Book makes no mention of a daughter born to Adam and Eve before Cain, so she must have been his younger sister, which made their union incestuous, but that was inevitable, given the circumstances.

The story of Cain and Abel poses more questions about the problem of good and evil than the story of the original sin. First there is the question that is always raised when we see the innocent victimized: why did God allow Cain to slay the good Abel? Wasn't he aware of what Cain was doing? And was Abel's tragic end the reward for his God-fearing virtue?

Genesis 4:19 informs us that "Lamech took unto him two wives." That means that polygamy was practiced among ancient Jews.

THE STORY OF NOAH

The story of Noah is a variation on the story of Adam. Noah fathered a new humanity, born after the flood had destroyed every living thing on earth except Noah's family and the creatures he took into his ark.

The flood to which this chapter of Genesis refers was very-likely a historical event which occurred in primeval times, for we find the same tale in the folklore of many peoples, from the Greeks to the Babylonians, as well as the Persians, Hindus, and some of the American Indian tribes. All of them believed the flood was a manifestation of God's wrath over the corruption of mankind;[1] the hero who was spared to build the ark and take into it those species from which a new creation would spring, had various names. The Greek legend of Deucalion and Pyrrha is well known. Deucalion, the son of Prometheus and husband of Pyrrha, was told to build an ark after Zeus had resolved to destroy the human race by flood. The ark floated for nine days and then came to rest on Mount Parnassus. Taken by itself, the tale is interesting as a legend invented to explain that world catastrophe, but it was later inserted into the Bible as part of the Scriptures. This story about the origin of mankind was accepted by untold millions throughout the centuries. Yet it is so full of holes, so ridiculously illogical, that one is embarrassed even to point out its inconsistencies.

Genesis 6:13–16: God tells Noah how to build the ark and specifies its dimensions. This anthropomorphic God has now become an expert carpenter, as he had been a tailor when he clothed Adam and Eve after they became aware of their nakedness and were ashamed of it.

The length of the ark was to be three hundred cubits, the breadth fifty, and the height thirty cubits. The Hebrew cubit was, according to some, only 18 inches; others say 20. Taking an average, in English measure, the ark's dimensions were: length 525 feet, breadth 87½ feet. Yet Chapter 6:19–21 enjoins Noah to take two of every creature on earth—one male and one female—plus all the food they would need, as well as food for himself and his wife, his sons and their wives. (There is no mention of any daughter Noah migh have had.)

First: how could he get so many animals into a ship of those dimensions? Second: Even if he could, how would he find them—two of every kind, male and female? Was he to search the globe, to cover every continent? And how would he catch them? Third: What was he to feed the carnivorous ones, such as lions and tigers? Would he give them the flesh of dead animals brought along for that purpose, or would he feed them live animals? Fourth: Supposing he could have done that, where would he have kept the animals? In cages? The story makes no reference to this. Is it likely that animals admitted to the ark would be quiet and docile when it was their instinct to prey upon each other? Fifth: The flood could drown land animals, but those in the sea were not only safe, but must have reveled in it. Sixth: How could Noah and his family bear to live with all those animals for 150 days?

Genesis 8:15–22: God again blessed mankind as he had done

for Adam, and promised he would not "curse the ground for man's sake; for the imagination of man's heart is evil from his youth; neither will I again smite any more everything living, as I have done." The Lord, who had smelled a sweet savor on earth, understood the beauty and sanctity of life; he suddenly felt, as Albert Schweitzer would put it, reverence for life, and was sorry he had destroyed it for man's sake. All living creatures, as well as plants, had been punished for man's wickedness. This glaring anthropocentric thinking the Lord now repudiated. In this chapter God behaves like a person who cannot control his anger and later regrets it. The consequence of God's ire was the destruction of all he had previously created. The earth, bare of life, lay before him, and he gazed at its ruin as a child looks upon the toy he has just smashed in a fit of temper. Then he promised he would never do it again, adding: "The imagination of man's heart is evil from his youth." This statement brings up a problem which has preoccupied theologians throughout the centuries. We wish to take issue with the above statement, for man's heart is not necessarily evil from youth; and usually it is not. However, Christians have been taught that man is corrupt, and continue to reiterate that we are all miserable sinners. Such a concept casts a shadow over all human life, and does much to destroy the joy of life.

There are some discrepancies in the text. Chapter 6, Verse 19 orders Noah to take two of every living thing, while Chapter 7, Verse 2 enjoins him to take of every clean beast by sevens, male and female; and of beasts that are not clean, by two, male and female; and "of fowls also of the air" (birds) by sevens, male and female. This contradiction between the two chapters indicates that the story of Noah was copied by different scribes or translators from different sources. As to clean and unclean animals, no definition for these has been given in the Book so far.

Chapter 9:6: "Whoso sheddeth blood, by man shall his blood be shed." This is the basis of legislation that requires an eye for an eye. It is elementary justice, but it is simplistic and brutal. It was practiced in England until fairly recent times, except that no blood was shed because murderers were hanged. The principle of a life for a life has long been debated, and in many countries, the death penalty is a subject that is constantly being reviewed.

After the flood, Noah settled down to become a farmer. He tilled the land, planted vine, and drank the fruit of the vine. One day, his youngest son went to his tent and found him in a drunken stupor, and stark naked. When he told his brothers about it, Shem and Japhet went to cover their father's nakedness. And Noah, awakened, cursed Ham (and his descendants) for what he had done to him. This is the biblical story, which is rather bewildering. Ham might have covered Noah and said nothing. Instead, he humiliated his father by telling his brothers about it, and the two of them covered his shame.

What was he ashamed of? Not of his drunkenness, but of being naked. Just as Adam and Eve were ashamed of their nakedness, after they had eaten the fruit of the forbidden tree. This is a second clue to the parallel between Adam and Noah. Both Adam, the father of mankind, and Noah, his late descendant, and father of a new mankind, commit the original sin, which is related to sex. The mention of Noah's nakedness suggests that he had indulged in some sexual orgy during his drunkenness.

This episode corroborates the Christian doctrine that all human existence is bound up with sin. We must therefore live to expiate that sin. In Sartre's *The Flies,* children, in fear and dread, apologize for being born, for even existing. Such a doctrine strengthened the domination of the Church. Priests had the power to absolve the sinner from the consequences of his sins, to make him clean again until the next confession. An easy and ingenuous device for learning people's secrets so as to control them.

THE TOWER OF BABEL

This chapter warns us against human effort that is too ambitious. Man should not try to exceed his natural limitations.

43

Goethe said, "Man should not tempt the gods." Yet, human history, all civilization, does exactly that. Man's constant effort is to transcend himself, to create something unheard of. Man dreams of actions, and tries to realize his dreams. Man challenges the laws of physics, aspires to what seems impossible, and the limits of the impossible recede as a result of his daring. Man wins his gamble with nature, but he also pays the price for it. The confusion of tongues to which this story refers can be interpreted symbolically: the more man extends his enterprises, the more miracles he performs, the less he understands his fellow men. And one could add: the less he understands himself. In modern terms: Technology is running away with us.

Babel is an allusion to Babylon. The Tower of Babel is the Babylonian ziggurat, or skyscraper of the time, nearly 300 feet, or 7 to 8 stories high. It was built in the center of an area reserved for temples, and consisted of square blocks placed terrace-like, each story being somewhat narrower than the preceding one, and of a different color. At the top was a chamber where the Statue of Divinity was kept. According to the historian, Herodotus, there was also a bed in this chapel in which the god slept with mortal women. Was it merely a temple, or was it used for other purposes too? According to Diodorus of Sicily, the ziggurat was also an observatory where the priests studied celestial phenomena. The Tower of Babel in the Bible, or ziggurat, was built around 2000 B.C. and reconstructed about 500 B.C.

Genesis 11:1 says that "the whole earth was of one language and of one speech." This contradicts Chapter 10:5: "The Gentiles divided in their own lands, every one after his own tongue, after their families, in their nations. And, in this story about the confusion of human languages the Book of Genesis makes a statement that is contrary to what we know about the evolution of human speech. Languages are the product of climatic and environmental conditions, and are continuously modified by changes in the culture. Like living organisms, they are born, they grow, and eventually they die. And the scattering of humans over the whole earth could not be considered a punishment, but rather a blessing for mankind; for how could they have found food and the necessities of life, if all humans had remained in one single place?

THE STORY OF ABRAM (ABRAHAM)

In Abram's story too, we find many discrepancies and much that does not stand up under critical examination.

Upon the urging of the Lord (that God is in constant communication with humans is a claim still made by present religious leaders), Abram emigrates from Ur of the Chaldees into the land of Canaan (which was not yet a land of milk and honey), and on to Egypt. According to Genesis 12:4, he was seventy-five years old when he left his homeland. He was accompanied by his wife Sarai. We do not know how old she was at that time, we only know that she was barren, that she had born no children to him. Arriving in Egypt, Abram told Sarai: "I know that thou art a fair woman to look upon," and asked her to tell the Egyptians that she was his sister, not his wife, for he thought that if they knew the truth, they would kill him and take Sarai. But this stratagem failed, and they carried her off to the Pharaoh's harem (Genesis 12:15). Because he was pleased, the Pharaoh bestowed great wealth upon Abram. In plain English, this means that Abram sold his wife to save his own skin and to gain riches. But then Genesis 12:17 adds: "And the Lord plagued Pharaoh and his house with great plagues because of Sarai, Abram's wife." Why didn't the Lord prevent the Pharaoh from taking Sarai in the first place?

The Pharaoh called Abram and asked why he had lied to him about Sarai. How did the Pharaoh find out the truth? Who told him? Chapter 12:19: "Why saidst thou, She is my sister? So I might have taken her to me to wife?" This suggests that the Pharaoh had not touched Sarai while she lived in his house, which was very unlikely, for her beauty had been greatly praised by the princes who had brought her to him.

The Pharaoh was generous to Abram, allowing him to leave with his wife, and take with him all that he had previously been given. This is strange. It was cowardly of Abram to deny that he was Sarai's husband and to let the Egyptian princes take her to the Pharaoh's house. Had he been a man and confident that the Lord would come to his aid, he would have risked his life to defend Sarai. And the Lord approved of this conduct; God's role was merely to harass the Egyptian ruler in order to make him release Sarai. And the Pharaoh, who had been deceived by Abram (and the Lord), allowed Abram to go with all his wealth; he may even have bestowed new gifts on him.

The underlying idea of this story of Abram is that Abram, future father of the Jewish race, is an ally of the Jewish god, who protects him against foreign powers. There is no morality involved. The Lord protects Abram against everything and everyone who might threaten him. Abram and the Jewish people had a covenant with God, in the same way that a nation today has a defense pact with another nation.

Genesis 15:5: After his adventure in Egypt, the Lord promised Abram that his wife would bear him children, and that his descendants would inherit the land of Canaan (13:15). "For all the land which thou seest, to thee will I give it, and to thy seed forever"; but this is contradicted in 15:13: "And he (the Lord) said unto Abram, Know of a surety that thy seed shall be a stranger in a land that is not theirs, and shall serve them; and they shall afflict them four hundred years." And further on, 15:18, the Lord makes Abram another promise, "Unto thy seed I have given this land, from the river of Egypt unto the great river, the river of Euphrates." If the Jews were to recall this promise, inserted into the Book of Genesis as authentic, they could claim the teritory from Egypt to the Euphrates; that is a large part of the entire Middle East. Morally, the Christians would have to support this claim, since it is based on a covenant with God.

The Lord constantly mentions Abram's seed; yet, at that point (Chapter 15), Abram's wife is still barren. In 15:4, the Lord said to Abram: "He that shall come forth out of thine own bowels, shall be thine heir," a promise that her barrenness would come to an end. Sarai and Abram do not seem to trust that promise, for Abram impregnates the servant Hagar at the direct invitation of his wife, so that Abram can be sure of offspring.

Chapter 16 recounts a very human story. After Hagar had conceived by Abram, she felt superior to Abram's wife and despised her. Sarai complained to Abram and he told her to do what she wanted with the servant girl. And Sarai must have rudely castigated her, for Chapter 16:6 says that Hagar fled into the wilderness to avoid her. It took an angel to get her back into Abram's house. The "ménage à trois" was not without stormy scenes.

The purpose of the Hagar story is to introduce the illegitimate branch of the Abram family, which will play a special role in the history of the Jews. Incidentally, Abram was 86 years old when his first child was born. And it was born to a servant instead of his wife.

ABRAM AND ISAAC

Genesis 22:1–19: The Book of Genesis is the Jewish Odyssey; and, like the great work of Homer, it is full of stirring episodes. One of these is the story of Abram's willing sacrifice of his son, Isaac, in compliance with God's demand.

The cry that resounds throughout the history of the Jewish religion is the need to love the Lord, the God of Israel, who has special solicitude for his people. "Love him with all thy heart, with all thy soul." This appeal amounts to a commandment. And the Abram-Isaac episode illustrates the commandment. Abram was ready to sacrifice his son at God's command. Hence, every Jew should be prepared to do as much, to give all he has without questioning the reason for God's command.

The idea of a parent sacrificing his child to God, or to gods, in order to prove his faith can be found in the Greek legend of Agamemnon and Iphigenia. This sacrifice was consummated, if we are to believe the version that served as a source for the Oresteia of Aeschylus. Goethe treated the same material in a spirit similar to that which prevails in the Abram-Isaac story, except that the goddess Pallas abducts Iphigenia, wrapping her in a cloud and taking her from the sacrificial altar to the country of Aulis, where Iphigenia becomes her priestess.

Returning to the biblical story, it seems clear that this is one more illustration of a theme that runs throughout the Old Testament: Jews are the chosen people, whose God will protect and guide them. This Jewish God is a powerful ally, but he is also a jealous God who demands, in return for his help, absolute obedience from his people.

THE STORY OF JACOB AND ESAU

Chapters 25 to 50 of the Book offer us an insight into the mentality of the times—the customs, morality, and ideals which prevailed then. Again there is emphasis on the alliance between God and the Jewish people. The Jews will become Israelites and Jacob will earn this name in the course of his adventures.

In Chapter 25, starting with Verse 23, we are told about Jacob's background. His mother, Rebecca, gave birth to twins, Esau and Jacob. Esau was first to emerge from his mother's womb, and therefore had the birthright of the firstborn. The Book remarks that he was redskinned and that his body was quite hairy; the implication is that, by contrast, Jacob's skin was white and smooth. At the birth of the twins, the Lord said to Rebecca (Verse 23), "Two nations are in thy womb, and two manner of people shall be separated from thy bowels; and the one people shall be stronger than the other people, and the elder shall serve the younger."

These words, attributed to God, really express human belief that the white race is superior to darker ones, and destined to rule over them. What better source could racists find for justificaton of their theory than this passage in the Book of Genesis? Certain peoples are born to be slaves and others to be masters; this is God's will.

While they were growing up, an incident occurred which appeared to confirm the Lord's prophecy. Esau had come home tired and hungry from his work in the fields and asked Jacob for some pottage. Jacob said, "Sell me this day thy birthright," and Esau, who placed little value upon it, agreed to sell the birthright for a pottage of lentils. This ignoble act is presented as a laudable one, because it conformed to God's will that the younger should become the founder of the master race. Taking advantage of other people's distress, as Jacob did, is part of a whole arsenal of weapons which the strong will use against the weak. The subsequent story underlines this belief. Outwitting the other fellow in order to prevail over him is a virtue extolled in the verses that follow.

Chapter 25:34 says: "then Jacob gave Esau bread and pottage of lentils; and he did eat and drink, and rose up, and went his way: thus Esau despised his birthright." The last part intimates that Esau deserved to be deprived of his birthright, because he was ready to sell it, and because he despised it. Moral: He who does not esteem his God-given right is not worthy of having it. Still, one wonders why God didn't cause Jacob to be born first, so that there would be no need for resorting to trickery.

Trickery is further extolled in Chapter 27:1–29. Having taken his birthright away from Esau, Jacob also wanted what went with it, namely, his father's blessing. His father, Isaac, loved Esau, but Rebecca, his mother, preferred Jacob and helped him obtain what he was after—the fatherly sanction of his birthright. Isaac was very old and nearly blind; Rebecca gave Jacob his brother's clothes and told him to cover his hands with goatskin so that Isaac, feeling them, should believe he was Esau, the hairy son. Isaac blessed Jacob. The magic of fatherly blessing was apparently believed by the author, or authors of the Book to be a powerful support, necessary for the conquest of life. As soon as Jacob obtained it, he departed and Esau arrived. He discovered Jacob's trickery and told his father. Isaac was stunned, but he could not help the situation. The magic of the blessing was spent; Jacob would become the master and Esau and Esau's offspring would serve him. Desperately, Esau asked whether his father could do something for him. Jacob predicted that Esau's descendants would one day free themselves from bondage by the sword, an ominous prophecy for Jacob's descendants, the white race. Esau hated his brother because of what he had done, and Rebecca, fearing for Jacob's life, advised him to leave. This was the beginning of many adventures for Jacob, including a struggle with his uncle, Laban, Rebecca's brother.

JACOB AND LABAN

Laban offered hospitality to his nephew, realizing that he was good at raising cattle and sheep. He offered him wages if he would stay and work for him. Jacob fell in love with Rachel, the younger daughter of Laban. He asked for her hand. "She will be yours if you serve me for seven years," Laban told him. Seven years of waiting would tax the patience of most lovers, but Jacob consented and the Book does not say that Rachel objected. But when the seven years were over, Laban got Jacob intoxicated and smuggled Leah, his older daughter, into his bed. When he awoke in the morning, poor Jacob, finding himself deceived, cried out: "What is this thou hast done unto me? Did not I serve with thee for Rachel? Wherefore hast thou then beguiled me?" (29:25). Laban justified his deception by saying that it was not customary in the country to marry off the younger daughter before the elder one. If Jacob wanted Rachel, too, he would have to serve for seven more years. What was he to do? He complied, harboring feelings of resentment and plans for revenge. Laban also gave Rachel to Jacob for wife and he served Laban for seven more years. Of course, there was jealousy and rivalry between the two sisters, sharing the same husband. Leah had several children, while Rachel remained barren. Rachel invited Jacob to lie with her servant, who would give him children in her stead; an extraordinary substitution, which repeats the story of Abram and Sarai, before the Lord opened Sarai's womb at a late age.

The purpose of inserting such episodes can only be surmised: they point to the fact that certain tribes of the Israelites are descendants of servant girls, and therefore destined always to remain members of the lower classes in Jewish society, much as the castes in India were, and still are, thought to be subordinated by divine will. This theory is borne out by the continuation of Rachel's story. God finally gave her children, one of whom was Joseph, who will play an outstanding role in our Book.

The time came for Jacob to return to his father's house. He asked Laban to release him and to give him due compensation for his long labor. It was previously agreed that Jacob would receive the speckled and spotted cattle and the brown sheep of the flock, which had increased greatly under his stewardship. This agreement had given Jacob the opportunity he was waiting for, a chance to take revenge on his father-in-law for the deceitful manner in which he had treated him. Chapters 30 and 35–43 explain: "He fed the cattle with rods of green poplar, and of the hazel of the chestnut tree, and piled white strakes in them, and made the white appear which was in the rods. He did this with the stronger cattle, while he let the feeble ones conceive plain brown offspring; so his own share grew, while Laban's diminished. And when he saw that his scheme worked, he fled clandestinely. Laban pursued him, but God appeared to him on the way and enjoined him to say nothing unkind to Jacob" (31–24). When he overtook Jacob, the son-in-law explained: he had been a faithful guardian of Laban's flock for twenty years. Ten times Laban had changed his wages, cheating him every time. He knew that he would never get permission to leave simply by asking. Laban would not have let him go. So he was forced to cut and run.

Laban had no answer to this; he had to let him go, not daring to attack him, because of God's warning.

Jacob and Esau's Story, Resumed

In Chapters 32 and 33 we come back to the story of Jacob's relationship with Esau, which was interrupted by Jacob's departure. Jacob sent messengers to Esau informing him of his imminent return. They came back with the news that Esau was coming to meet him and was bringing along four hundred men. This news filled Jacob with fear. He remembered how he had cheated his brother out of his birthright and of their father's blessing. He had every reason to expect Esau's vengeance. He divided his flock, letting the women and children go with part of it, so that if Esau attacked him they would not be hurt. Yet, to his amazement, Esau came and embraced him, greeting him as a brother. Truly, the nobility of Esau stands out in this incident. He had forgiven the wrongs which were done to him. He refused the many sheep and goats and other presents which Jacob offered him to placate his anger. He finally accepted them graciously, as any man might accept gifts from a brother who had been away.

A SAVAGE EPISODE

Chapter 34 constitutes a tale of extreme cunning and savagery. In Canaan, where Jacob had stopped for a while during the journey to his father's house, a young man fell in love with one of Leah's daughters. He led her away and enjoyed her love, and afterwards proposed to marry her. A simple story which should have ended happily. The girl's family and entourage invited their guests to join them, and together they would be as one family. The sons of Jacob accepted, on condition that all males among their hosts be circumcised so as to be like them. The hosts consented—an extraordinary proof of their good intentions. On the third day after these wholesale operations, when the pain from them was the most intense, two of the girl's brothers attacked the suffering men. They took advantage of their weakened condition to slaughter them. Then they took women and children captive, looted the houses, and destroyed what they could not take with them. All this to avenge the affront to their sister.

And the narrator obviously believes that this bloody deed was noble and praiseworthy because it was done to protect a woman's virtue!

JACOB'S LADDER AND STRUGGLE WITH THE ANGEL

Jacob had two strange adventures. The first was a dream (Chapter 28:12). He saw "a ladder set up on the earth, and the top of it reached to heaven: and behold the angels of God ascending and descending it."

The Lord stood at the top and promised Jacob he would give him the land on which he lay, and that his descendants would be numerous as the dust of the earth. The Lord also vowed to support and sustain him in all his enterprises.

Jacob's second adventure was his struggle with an angel, who came down to earth in human form and wrestled with Jacob all night. Jacob was clearly stronger, for when dawn came, the angel begged to be released. Jacob agreed on condition that he receive a blessing.

The two adventures are connected. Both symbolize God's alliance with Jacob, renamed Israel; his alliance with the people of Israel. As the angel puts it: "as a prince hast thou power with God and with men, and hast prevailed." His people will be henceforth called the Israelites, that is, the allies of God, the chosen people who have a covenant with God.

God is the father of his people and Jacob is his prophet.

The Book of Genesis ends with a tale that contains a profound truth and a message, namely, that jealousy, wickedness, and hatred can be overcome by pure and unselfish love.

Joseph is clearly an ideal hero, destined for great things. He is a dreamer, the preferred child of his father, God's delight. His brothers are jealous of him; they decide to kill him, but he must be saved if God's design is to be accomplished: A caravan of merchants passes by and the brothers decide to sell him into slavery and make a profit from the deal.

Joseph has no defense other than his innocence and the beauty of his youth. He is brought to Egypt and sold to an officer of the Pharaoh. The officer's wife falls in love with him, but Joseph refuses to betray the master who has been good to him. The story of Joseph and the wife of Potiphar has been cited innumerable times as an example of innocence slandered. It may have been borrowed from Hyppolitus, in which Euripides tells the same story. And this theme was used later in Phèdre, a French tragedy. In every case, the rejected woman produces evidence of the young man's treachery, and the husband, who believes her, punishes the victim of his wife's lust.

Joseph is thrown into prison, but is saved by the Lord, who has endowed him with the gift of interpreting dreams. Joseph explains the Pharaoh's dream about the seven fat kine, devoured by the seven lean ones. Thanks to his foresight, Egypt manages to feed her own people during the seven lean years, and even to save others from famine. Among these are Joseph's father, Israel (Jacob) and his own brothers. And the tale ends as it should; greatness of heart is rewarded, Israel retrieves the favorite son he had mourned. He rejoices also in the two sons of Joseph, born in Egypt. Joseph, second only to the Pharaoh in Egypt, lived happily ever after till the age of one hundred and ten. But the children of Israel were, after his death, enslaved by the Egyptians, until God gave them a new leader, Moses, who led them out from slavery into the land of milk and honey that Canaan had become.

And the message in Joseph's story, namely, that love is stronger than might, heralds the coming message of Christ, which will eventually conquer the Roman Empire.

CREATION VERSUS EVOLUTION

The preceding reflections have not been set forth to deride the biblical text. Nothing was further from the author's intention. He wished only to point out how impossible is its fundamentalist, literal interpretation. The seven days that, the text says, it took the Lord to create this earth of ours with its oceans, its land surface, its innumerable creatures, from protozoa to amoeba, all the way up to humans, represent, according to now known scientific data, between thirty to sixty billion years.

Arthur Thompson, who delivered the first lectures initiated by the Dwight Harrison Terry Foundation of Yale University about evolution, and author of the book *Concerning Evolution,* says: "It is a human peculiarity, occasionally endearing, but more often maddening, that no amount of proof suffices to convince those who simply do not want to know or to accept the truth." He went on to say, "Of course, there are some beliefs still current, labeled as religions and involved in religious emotions, that are flatly incompatible with evolution and that therefore are intellectually untenable in spite of their intellectual appeal. Nevertheless, I take it now self-evident, requiring no further discussion, that evolution and true religion are compatible."[2]

These comments are especially relevant today because of the intellectually untenable theses that have been brought forward by religious zealots who simply will not accept the truth. In order to combat the scientifically established data about the evolution of mammals, and among these the evolution of certain primates to man, they have invented a pseudoscience which they call "scientific creation." The battle which took place during the Scopes trial of 1925, which condemned a school teacher for exposing his students to Darwin's theory about the evolution of the species, has begun again. Fundamentalists consider it sacrilegious to say that man has evolved from the apes. Supporters of "scientific creation" ignore the discovery of hominid fragments; the latest bone fragments were found in Africa in 1978 and are estimated to be about three and a half million years old. Also ignored are thousands of stone tools used by an ancestor dubbed "Homo erectus," who lived around 1 milion to 1.5 million years ago. Additional finds include a skull roughly 300,000 years old and innumerable animal fossils, as well as fossil records established by radioactive decay and the records on rocks. Supporters of "scientific creation" are unable to produce anything equally reliable; their evidence must be taken on faith. It is useless to debate with them because they refuse to argue on rational grounds. Instead, they try to pressure state legislatures into making laws which would give equal rights to the teaching of their theory along with evolution. Worse, they promulgate the idea that evolution is the speculative theory of a single mind and merely one of several scientific hypotheses about life on earth. Ultraconservatives prevent their children from learning about evolution by withdrawing them from public schools; they are taught the Biblical text only. There are those who suggest that to deny the Biblical story of creation is to deny the word of God; they say it is the mark of atheistic humanism and sympathy with communism.

All of this is distressing. If legislatures listen to these people, they are helping to obfuscate young minds, to make them impervious to reason. This is detrimental to our country, which is thus deprived of potentially able scientists. Such a viewpoint is detrimental to religion itself, for it fosters a crude and ignorant interpretation of the Scriptures.

Life is spirit, intelligence breathed into matter. Every life is the expression of an idea of nature. The Creative Intelligence of the Universe begins with an idea. The originator of the idea likes to experiment with it, to infuse matter with it in various shapes, as an artist might make several sketches of one model, trying each time to improve the expression of his vision.

The Great Experimenter works with enthusiasm, creating subtypes from the general type, and further subtypes from these, allowing all of them to work out their own destiny. The spirit that is breathed into each will work constantly to perfect that individual type. A sudden new idea might prompt a rapid development, enriching the original idea; the carriers of this new idea will then eclipse former varieties. Evolution is usually slow, but as we have said, rapid and even sudden developments may occur. Sometimes, of course, the original idea is found adequate for the particular purpose it serves. Then the species will not evolve. It is like a good product which satisfies the clientele; there is no reason to change it.

Evolution means replacement of less perfect varieties with more perfect ones; this applies everywhere in nature; is there any reason to suppose that it's not applicable to humans? Man is a primate, a mammal and a chordate. In the humanoid class, apes have been replaced by "homo." It is ludicrous that this fact should be regarded as degrading to our species. If "homo" is the highest representative, or the highest expression of the original idea, which was to produce earth's most intelligent creature, we, as humans, should be proud and grateful that we were chosen for the role.

This role is a privileged one, but it entails responsibilities. The most fundamental change which has taken place since man's evolution from mammal to "homo" is that he now has the capacity to control his own evolution. (This, by the way, might lead to the evolution of other species under his direction.) Man's responsibility is awesome. His manipulations could produce individuals destined to perform servile tasks or even criminal ones. On the other hand, he might create men capable of marvelous and sublime undertakings. It is now only a matter of perfecting his ability to alter nature and bend it to his own purposes.

But in order to survive in geological terms and to make this planet livable, man must use his great ingenuity and intelligence for the betterment of all living things. Sympathy for his fellow creatures, pity, and love which is not limited to his own kind are the distinguishing characteristics of man.

SCIENCE MERGES WITH RELIGION

Science leads us to recognition of the unity of the human species. As we penetrate deeper and deeper into the evolutionary process and the way it works, we reach certain conclusions about mankind and life in general. Like religion, science looks beyond the short earthly life of the individual. Science, however, arrives at its conclusions not by means of divine revelation but by making use of spirit, the source of all understanding, of all creation and discovery. His ability to learn has enabled man to discover that he is as much a product of evolution as any other creature. This conclusion confirms the religious principle of the oneness of life.

Like religion, science is able to admire the marvelous spectacle of Creative Intelligence at work. And science also acknowledges that this universal force, which vibrates and flourishes in all creatures, transcends the purely mechanistic operation of material life and is working toward a foreordained goal. This force not only negates, but reverses the material law of cause and effect by anticipating it. Thus the universe is irresistibly evolving toward this cosmic goal.

Chapter III

OF GOD AND MAN

The Jewish concept that God is One, the Almighty and the Creator of the Universe, was a revolutionary spiritual development and had a tremendous impact on the history and civilization of mankind. It was revolutionary because this Jewish God was not only One, but was also invisible and could not be represented by carved images placed in temples. Nations such as Egypt and Rome had been wont to cultivate many divinities in human or animal form. People believed that there were spirits dwelling in forests, rivers and other places, and these spirits had to be propitiated.

This God of the Jews, this single God was thought to be a stern judge who demanded absolute obedience. If the Chosen People kept His commandments, He would protect them from their enemies.

The Christians improved upon this concept by making the Almighty a God of love and the father of mankind; a father who sent His only begotten son to take upon himself the sins of men.

The Judeo-Christian faith led man to focus on One God rather than a multiplicity of spirits dwelling in nature. But actually it expanded his spiritual vision to see that all of nature was infused with this same universal spirit. By virtue of this belief man felt close to God and His creation; his whole life was permeated with spirit.

But if God was to be his guide and his law, his aspiration and inspiration, man had to know more; who was God? What was His design for man and what should man do to carry out this divine plan? Man's questions were deep and searching. Sometimes they were bold and challenging, often, they were humble. And the answers he received were various. Questions and answers were restated and renewed throughout the centuries, but failed to satisfy the thirst of man to know the Unknowable.

THE ESSENCE OF GOD

God is spirit. God is immanent, indwelling in the Universe. The Universe emanates from Him. The Creative Spirit of the Universe is the source of all life, creativity being of the Spirit. Man believes that he partakes of God's creative spirit, that he is the representative of divine creativity on earth.

Creativity is synonymous with causality, for any creator causes something to happen. God is the primary cause, the Prime Mover, as Aristotle called Him. Kant's definition: God is the source of all *a priori,* is the same as the source of all causality. This must be so, for if God were not eternal there would be a cause prior to him, and that prior cause would be God.

In ages when science was practically unknown, mythical explanations were given of the origin of the universe. The Book of Genesis says that God created the universe out of chaos. This implies that God, before creating the universe, did nothing for aeons but hover over chaos. Yet, to the human mind, God is equated with creativity.

We accept only one answer about the creation of the world, namely, that the universe has never been created, has eternally existed, because we cannot imagine nothingness. Even chaos is a universe in transformation. God's essence is creation, which is eternally at work.

God is immanent in nature but he is also transcending it. Christians see this duality, or state of being transcendent and immanent simultaneously, as one of those paradoxes we always encounter when speaking of God. In fact, the Creative Spirit must transcend creation, since the latter is emanating from it. Yet it is of the same essence, is infused with it.

60

Man, earth's most intelligent being, inherits this dual character; he is a creature, but he is also the creator of many things on this planet and even capable of altering the course of nature. Man comes closest to understanding God's being when he thinks of his own basic characteristic, which is independent creativity. Still, being a creature, he cannot help thinking of Him who was never a creature but always Creator and nothing else.

The very wish to understand God leads man to a higher existence, for his motive is to be like God, and he strives to imitate Him insofar as he knows how.

When man reaches out to the Supreme Being, he is trying to improve, to purify himself and prepare for his own transcendence.

THE ATTRIBUTES OF GOD

Man lifted his thoughts above earthly contingencies to conceive of a supremely intelligent being. Such soaring thoughts filled him with happiness before unknown; he tasted transcendence. He felt God in himself, was fused with Him. He sought words to express his new and blessed state, and thus enriched his speech to characterize the phenomenon taking place within. He invented words to name that superior being he now felt part of. It stretched his imagination to define it. Diverse religions, diverse philosophies, and thinkers everywhere have searched for superlatives to indicate the superhuman. But human language remains human and cannot adequately express the concept of Universal, Creative Spirit.

Thus our faculty for defining that spirit is limited. We see it as a person because it is ever-active. We call Him God, for we need a simple name to refer to Him. We think of His power and grope for adjectives, but these serve only to circumscribe His infinity. We say that he is Lord of the Universe, that He is immutable, unchanging, for if He should change, He would no longer be what He is. This does not apply to the universe, however, which is ever changing, for God's concept of unity is expressed as continual unfoldment. We call Him perfect, a word that eludes us and remains an abstraction. This epithet "perfect" expresses the gap between the divine and the human.

We call Him *omnipresent,* because if He is, He is unlimited, encompassing and infusing every creature and everything in this vast universe. We call Him *indivisible,* for though His spirit is diffused, this diffusion is the very condition of creation.

Thus God and His creation are a synthesis of opposites, for He is infinite while His creatures are limited, by nature; by their individual capacities, as well as by environment and circumstance.

God is all powerful, but He cannot change, has no freedom to be other than He is. His will is law even unto Him. Freedom is uncertainty; God is absolute certainty. Freedom entails the anguish of choice, whereas God is serene. That God has freedom is an illusion, but He Himself is not an illusion, not as man conceives of Him. God knows Himself, He is subject and object to Himself, and we as humans, try to approximate this completeness in our efforts to acquire self-knowledge. God is the point of departure of causality, for all happenings derive from Him. He is also the end of causality, for all happenings end in Him. God is mind and the source of all intelligence. He is life because intelligence is creative. God is eternal, because intelligence never ceases to be active in the Cosmos. We equate intelligence with life, therefore we must conclude that God, or creative intelligence, has endowed all individual creatures and all things with an inherent will to assert their own particular natures. Oceans breathe and we call their breathing tides. Trees bleed if they are wounded, and certain flowers withdraw if they are touched. Others close their petals up at nightfall, as birds fold their wings to sleep. We say that God is holy, good, and just, but these human terms do not apply to nature, which is indifferent.

God is *omniscient.* His intelligence embraces and retains all

that has happened or will happen in the universe. yet all creatures are endowed with free will. This contradiction has baffled
thinkers and theologians for centuries. No one has come up
with an acceptable solution to this enigma.

God is *simple* because he is primal essence and will, though
His simplicity is above, superior to man's complexity. God is
both *potentiality* and *actuality* and each is infinite. He is *en-
telechy,* fulfillment, fulfilled in His own perfection. God is *one
and only one,* for infinite perfection has no peer. Christians
say, "God is invisible, but He made Himself visible in His son,
Jesus Christ."

All of the attributes which we confer upon Him are like
arrows that fall short of their target. We cannot penetrate his
Being and so have no means of determining what He is like.

Religions have given God various names, such as Adonai,
Jehovah, Allah, or The Lord, but to name Him at all is degrading, an attempt to bring Him down to our level. We try to
encompass Him with our limited intelligence, which is impossible. This is why preachers and religious teachers say we
should not speak of God lightly or profane His name. People
in general feel this too, and often use other words coined for
the purpose, such as "gosh" or "golly," which have a similar
sound.

His concept of God is the noblest, loftiest image man has of
himself, of what he aspires to be. In conceiving God, man has
envisioned his own transcendence.

THE PROOFS OF GOD'S EXISTENCE

Ever since the concept of one invisible God first took shape
in man's mind, he has been haunted by the need to believe that
this God really exists. God's existence must be proven, not only
to persuade doubters, but also to satisfy believers. For those
who are great believers have been, at times, great doubters.
And to doubt has filled men with terror and sadness, for they

needed to believe. The brilliant Pascal, for instance, gave up science to proclaim the glory of God; proof of his inner torment was later revealed in this statement: "It is impossible that God exists and it is unconceivable that He does not exist." Another, and even more poignant example was the Russian writer, Dostoevsky. The duel between his reason and his longing for God turned out to be an inexhaustible source of artistic inspiration. The problem, as we have seen, is this: if man believes in God's omnipotence and omniscience, then he must conclude that God knows in advance what man will do, or decide to do, at any given moment. In other words, man's whole life is predetermined, which means that freedom of action is illusory. If God exists and possesses the attributes which religion claims for Him, then man is nothing but God's puppet.

In Dostoevsky's novel, *The Possessed,* Kirilov is determined to prove that he can free himself from God's control. He decides to kill himself, believing that this will be an act of free will. But his natural instinct for self-preservation causes him to delay in carrying out this resolution. Finally, manipulated by young Verkovensky, a demoniac figure, he is driven to suicide. But having killed himself while in a state of insanity, he was not in control and has failed to prove his point.

If representatives of the major religions are asked to prove God's existence, they become evasive. This is only natural. Nevertheless, attempts have been made to come up with logical arguments which would satisfy the queries of skeptics.

The Ontological Proof

God must exist because man needs Him, and because he has conceived of such a Being. This stirring of the Divine within man is the affirmation of God. The fact that man has thought of this divine idea is proof of the existence of The Divine.

So goes the ontological argument. It is both rational and emotional. Rational because Pascal and Leibniz have shown us the infinity of the Cosmos and the infinitesimal beings which swarm around us, visibly or invisibly. We have seen that these, however minute, are subject to the same laws as giant galaxies. Once we understand that individual creatures as well as worlds are ruled by these laws, we cannot avoid the conclusion that creation is the work of a Supreme Intelligence, of a Great Physicist and Organizer. And we see that creation is going on continuously according to some master plan.

Arriving at the ontological proof, however, is an emotional process. We are influenced by the desire to have our reason conjure up the Supreme God, that Perfect Being which we long for.

But reason rebels. It says, "How can I believe in a Being that is invisible, that always remains hidden?" Then it answers its own objection, "Can there be creation without a Creator? *Ex nihilo nihil.*"

The ontological argument is more forceful than any other, either philosophical or theological, which aims at proving God's existence.

One variety of ontological proof is that which says: "God Is a Necessity." This is called the principle of sufficient reason. Looking around us, we see birds and insects, lions and jackals, fish in the sea. Man is one of countless creatures living on this planet. Surrounding it are constellations of stars, our solar system, and numberless galaxies. How did all this come about? The obvious answer is that some Master Mind has created it. If we and the universe have any meaning, there must be a God who has expressed Himself through His creation. We and the world exist, according to this argument, by the principle of sufficient reason. Our existence obtains its meaning from God. Denying God, man becomes a meaningless creature in a vast universe. Therefore, God is a necessity.

This argument deprives us of independence. But faced with such immensity, we are nothing, less than the worms, unless we acknowledge God as our author and play the role He has assigned to us in the universal drama.

If we accept the argument of sufficient reason, all becomes harmonious, everything falls into place and the puzzle is solved.

If we deny it, we will be like Sisyphus, who continually assaulted the abode of the gods and was eternally frustrated, eternally punished. We will be orphans, pariahs in the universe.

The God of the Saints

The Church fathers, like ordinary mortals, wrestled with the problem of God. Saint Paul founded his faith on the works of Jesus Christ, the Redeemer. His reasoning went as follows: God sent his Son into the world to save humanity. Jesus endured crucifixion, which in the Roman world was reserved for criminals. He bowed to the Divine Will, though it meant agony and humiliation, acknowledging his Sonship even from the cross. His selfless love was an expression of the Divine love which embraces all mankind. What further proof is needed of the divine order and the universal Father who has created it?

Saint Augustine, who, like Paul, was an ardent defender of the faith after his conversion, felt no need to "prove" that God exists. He chose, rather, to believe in Him as the first step toward knowing the Truth. He said, "I believe in order to know," whereas Descartes would have said, "I want to know in order to believe." Saint Augustine willingly and fervently accepted the authority of the Church. "I would not believe in the Gospel if I were not moved to do so by the authority of the Church." His monumental work, "The City of God," was founded upon deep conviction.

Saint Augustine's faith was not the easy solution of someone tired of reasoning, who accepts a ready-made truth from others. His was an artistic and sensitive nature, readily overwhelmed by the beauty of creation.

> Ask the loveliness of the earth, ask the loveliness of the sea, ask the loveliness of the wide airy spaces, ask the loveliness of the sky, ask the order of the stars, ask the sun making the day light with its beams, ask the moon tempering the darkness of the night that follows, ask the living things which move in the waters, which tarry on the land, which fly in the air; ask the

souls that are hidden, the bodies that are perceptive; the visible things which must be governed, the invisible things which govern: ask all these things, and they will all answer thee, Lo, see we are lovely. Their loveliness is their confession. And these lovely but mutable things, who has made them, save Beauty immutable?[1]

Isn't it natural that the beauty of unfolding life, the majesty of universal laws, and the ordered movement of celestial bodies should inspire men with awe? That nature's blessings should move them to worship their Creator, and renounce all further speculation? Saint Augustine and later Pascal found peace and satisfaction in this way. They solved the problem of God's existence for themselves. Saint Augustine's solution was: "You must believe." It had meaning for him that was based on his love for the beauty and symmetry in nature. This is not to say that he ignored the mental process or the rationale. It was his reason which convinced him that only the existence of a Creator could account for the beauty and order around us.

THE FIVE PROOFS OF ST. THOMAS AQUINAS

St. Thomas Aquinas found God, not by relinquishing his reason, but rather by making full use of it. He came up with five arguments to prove God's existence. His conclusions are actually variations of those which others had arrived at before him.

His first argument, for instance, echoes Plato and Aristotle: All things move, but there must be a Prime Mover. The second is similar to the first and is based on causality: All things are effects and must therefore have a cause. Climbing from cause to cause, we arrive at the Primary Cause—we call it God.

His third argument harks back to the old argument of sufficient reason: All things eventually perish; yet life goes on. Nature reproduces these and other things at will; this process of renewal is continuous. But none of these things could exist

67

if there were not a source of life which never perishes. This indispensable source, which is anterior to all things and completely self-sustaining, we call God.

The fourth argument is in a similar vein: All things possess certain qualities. They possess them to a greater or lesser degree, so that, in the human realm, all is relative. But as we move upward in the scale of perfection, we arrive at the ultimate, at a point which is unsurpassable. This state of absolute perfection is God.

The fifth argument postulates that intelligence pervades the universe. All creatures show intelligence in that they try to survive. The spider spins its web to capture the food it needs; the tree sends sap toward its branches and leaves; the leaves open in such a way as to absorb life-sustaining moisture. Intelligence is manifested in the endless variety of ways and means that living creatures have invented to survive. Their intelligence, argues St. Thomas, is derived from the Sustainer of Life, from their Creator.

St. Thomas Aquinas believed in God because he undertook to prove his existence. This is characteristic of saints, and indeed, of all Christians. Philosophers, on the other hand, refuse to take an à priori attitude; they must be persuaded by logic. Faith does not rely on reason, and reason is also independent of faith, for it insists on making its own judgements, after it has weighed the evidence.

It is requisite that we should learn how those in the philosopher's camp, who are some of Western culture's most eminent minds, view the problem of creation and Creator.

Chapter IV

GOD AND THE PHILOSOPHERS

PLATO (SPEAKING THROUGH SOCRATES)

Socrates analyzes degrees of reality in objects accessible to man's knowledge. Shadows and reflections in water are of course the most transient and insubstantial, being but the pale counterparts of solid material objects. Beyond these objects, however, is the invisible world of perfect ideas, of which things in the visible imperfect world are in turn pale counterparts. And above all this multiplicity is that state of absolute harmony to which only the most highly trained human intelligence can soar.

> The prison house is the world of sight, the light of the fire is the sun, and you will not misapprehend me if you interpret the journey upwards to be the ascent of the soul into the intellectual world according to my poor belief, which, at your desire, I have expressed—whether rightly or wrongly, God knows. But, whether true or false, my opinion is that in the world of knowledge the idea of good appears last of all, and is seen only with an effort; when seen is inferred to be the universal author of all things beautiful and right, parent of light.[1]

It was reasoning that led Plato to the discovery of the First Cause, to the absolute Truth. The fact that reason can ascend to God proves that He is intelligence; and that He is the Supreme Good, for Supreme Intelligence would never create anything that was not consonant with the perfect harmony of its grand design. Thus, God is good, and all that is good leads to God. Plato often spoke of gods, yet he concluded that there was really only one Godhead, One Supreme Being. As we have said, it was intelligence which led him to this conclusion, for he

69

disregarded all revelation. Intelligent reasoning might seem to deprive God of mystery, were it not that the idea of intelligence as the creative principle is in itself a sublime mystery which we have yet to unravel.

ARISTOTLE

In his *Metaphysics,* Aristotle starts with the problem of being. Being is the result of changing inert matter through motion. That which produces the change is the cause, and the product, or form, is the effect. But every cause might also be called an effect since it was produced by a previous cause. Moving back along this chain of cause and effect, we eventually arrive at the first cause, established by Plato and Socrates.[2] This original cause is by definition immovable and unchanging, for motion is change. It is pure thought, thinking itself, and perfect tranquility. To reiterate, the first cause has never been moved and never changes; thus it never had a beginning.[3]

Given the immutability of the Prime Mover, Aristotle reasoned that the universe never had a beginning, either. It has always been and has continually renewed itself. It is in perpetual motion. *The* universe had no beginning; only *a* universe has a beginning and an end through change. With extraordinary vision, Aristotle advances the theory of a changing universe and concomitantly that of eternal recurrence within it. Thus, two eternal laws govern the universe: change and decay on the one hand, eternal renewal on the other.[4]

Nothing is moved at random; there must always be something to move it, even as things are moved in one way by Nature, and in another by force, by mind, or by something else.

Therefore there was no infinite age of Chaos and Night, for the same things have always existed, either revolving in a cycle or moving in some other mode, as the actual is prior to the potential. If the same is constantly repeating itself in cycles, there must be something always active there in the same way.

70

There must always be a repetition. If there is birth and death there must be always something active there in two different ways . . . And the first is the cause of what is permanent and the second of what is different, and both together are the causes of perpetual variation. Now then, this is just the character of our motion. Why then do we need to look for more principles?

"If there has never been a beginning of *the* Universe . . . it is impossible that motion should ever have begun or should ever have come to an end, for it has always been perpetual. Time never had a beginning either, for there could never have been a before or an after if time did not exist.

"Time is a continuous flow . . . it is intrinsic to the universe." And Aristotle adds, "Motion, then, is forever continuous, as time is, for time is either *the same as motion or a condition of motion.*"[5] In this last sentence Aristotle laid down a theory which was to be developed twenty-five hundred years later by Einstein. He called it the Theory of Relativity.

For brief moments man is in harmony with God's being. He is most at one with this Mind when he contemplates the universe and thinks about his relationship to it. Then he becomes both a subject thinking and an object of thought. This happy state of mind which we sometimes achieve has its origin in God, for He is, in fact, that perfect state of mind which we strive for.

Life, too, belongs to God, for thought as actuality is life, and God is that actuality.

God being perfect, His creation, the actuality of His thoughts, must be good. This idea was later repeated by Leibnitz. "God's actuality is most good and everlasting. We say then that God is a living being, eternal, most good. And so life and unbroken and eternal existence are God's for this is God."[6]

SENECA

The Roman philosopher Seneca, during whose lifetime Christianity spread throughout the Roman Empire, spoke of gods, as was customary in his day; but his reason led him to the One God, the Supreme Master of the Universe.

He was a deep thinker and a student of nature who was seeking the origin of all things, or what the Greeks called *tò ón*. The Romans referred to it as *quod est,* while the Germans used the word *Urwesen.* Seneca equated this original cause with God.

Quod est includes the animate and inanimate world. This idea of a pristine cause was formulated by the human mind. The very fact that man was capable of such an idea might be considered proof of God's existence. This is what is called the ontological proof.

Seneca was absolutely certain that the mighty structure of the universe could not exist without a caretaker. The laws that regulate the movement of celestial bodies, their order and their constellations, must derive from a central intelligence.

"The concourse and dispersal of the heavenly bodies are not an effect of fortuitous impulse," he says in his treatise *Of Providence.*

Seneca then quotes Plato, "The Ideal Being who is immortal and immutable, is constantly at work in nature."

When Seneca speaks of gods, the concept means to him the division of the Universal Spirit, divided but One, and present in all creation.

One of his *Fragments (No. 6)* for instance, contains the following words: "When He (God) drew up his plans and laid down the building stones for His magnificent edifice which is the most perfect in all nature, He was looking for leaders; and even though *He Himself merged with the totality of His creation,* He created the gods to supervise his work."[7]

This quotation presents the Creator as the Supreme Being; under Him there are spirits which assure the perfect fulfillment and functioning of the divine plan. The quotation implies, therefore, a certain hierarchy in the ranks of the spirits, similar to the Christian theological hierarchy. The gods appointed by the Supreme Being would, in Seneca's mind, correspond to the angels. And man could be classified as ranking immediately under them. This is suggested in *Fragment No. 7* when he says, "Our thoughts come to us from beings who inspire what is best in us."

The words quoted earlier, "He merged with the totality of His creation," have a pantheistic connotation, corroborated by *Fragment No. 11*: "Shall we praise God less because He has placed His power in nature? No, we shall praise Him because He gave us nature, *for nature is the same as God.*"

Nature is a fountain of eternal marvels to this philosopher. He admires the diversity of things within their greater similarity; all creatures belong to certain classes or species, yet each of them is different from every other. The human mind can encompass only a tiny portion of this vast universe, but God is present in our thought, though we cannot see Him. Seneca's idea of an invisible God, an only God and Creator, was very close to that of Jews and Christians, but it must have been startling to the Romans of that day who carved images of their gods and those of other peoples, and were used to having them in their temples.

Seneca praises this invisible God in words that read like a hymn: "What is a God? All that you see and do not see. His greatness exceeds our imagination. He alone is All, His own work within and without."

He is what you see and don't see. God is therefore omnipresent. And He is within us, we are part of His being.

Seneca shares Plato's view that God is good, and because He is good, the world He created is the best possible world. It is an argument that originates with the Stoics; later it was professed by Leibnitz and satirized by Voltaire in *Candide*.

The rational part of the human soul directs our life toward God. God is the supreme good, consequently all that is good comes from Him.

This belief, namely, that good is of divine origin, is contrary to the idea that good and evil are relative. For Seneca, good and evil are absolute values. Evil is for him that which does

73

not come from God, when man strays from the dictates of his reason.

In the light of the above, one can understand why the Christians felt close enough to Seneca to call him *noster,* "our Seneca."

Seneca's eye delights in the incomparable beauty, variety, and greatness of nature: He is impatient with people who maintain that all is accident, denying that there is a creator behind the creation. How can they fail to see that all is reason, that the movement of the planets, the life of animals and humans, the law inherent in all life, the storms, clouds and all phenomena, are regulated according to a grand design? How can they believe that all this is due to some blind force and that nature does not know what it is doing? And he deplored the fact that such misconceptions are adopted not only by the uneducated, but even by well educated people.

Seneca studied natural phenomena to better understand the nature of God. The preface to the first book of his *Natural Questions* concerns itself with metaphysics; his research and conclusions are imbued with philosophical speculation. God is the beginning and the end of Seneca's philosophy.

LUCRETIUS

Lucretius was a poet, a philosopher and a naturalist. He is seen at a distance of twenty centuries as a lonely and tormented figure; a man of solid convictions which he was impelled to share with others so as to enlighten them, to free them from the fear of death and from judgment beyond the grave.

His work has been lost, except one long poem in hexameters, entitled "Of the Nature of Things" *(De Natura Rerum)* made up of six parts. The poet endeavors to unload his burden, the secret which he has discovered after constant soul searching and deep study had caused him to reject prevailing views and prejudice. The subjects he treats are those which have been important to every age. He deals with questions which every generation, indeed, every individual, poses anew: questions about the formation of the world, about the soul and mind, about life and death, as well as life after death, and finally, about God.

The poet's personal philosophy is expounded in the fifth part of the poem. This sentence summarizes it: "The Universe is formed of a mortal body and at the same time it had birth." In other words, everything, the oceans, our planet, the solar system, stars and galaxies, are living beings that are born, develop, and die. "See you not that even stones are conquered by time, that high towers fall and rocks moulder away, that shrines and idols of gods fall into decay, and that the holy divinity cannot exceed the bonds of fate or struggle against the fixed laws of nature?" He denies that our planet was planned and created by God. "For, verily, not by design did the first beginnings of things find their right places by keen intelligence."

The first beginnings of earth were due to what the author calls "mighty blows for infinite ages,"[8] cosmic forces that brought diverse elements together which then coalesced, after some trial and error, to form a whole. The earth, then, had its origin in the play of cosmic forces. Once constituted, the earth fostered life and the evolution of life on its surface. Because the earth is the mother of life, we call it Mother Nature. Nothing fell from Heaven. Many races have been born on earth, but only the strongest have survived. "For in the case of every species which is still alive, either speed, or craft or courage has protected and preserved them since their birth." This quotation sounds like a paraphrase of Darwin's "survival of the fittest." As soon as they had managed to subdue the animals and protect themselves from the elements, men began to organize communities. This was for mutual protection and safety. To further secure their existence, they established codes of law which they pledged themselves to obey. After arriving at that stage of civilization, man created the gods. The reason for their creation, says Lucretius, was that man needed to have beings more marvelous and more powerful than himself to emulate, and his imagination supplied them. Thus the gods owe their existence to man's desire for transcendence.

The fear of death is concomitant with a belief in gods and future punishment, for no one feels that his life has been entirely free of guilt.

There was another reason, besides his need for transcendence, why man had to invent superhuman powers. This was his ignorance and fear of natural phenomena. We are tempted to call this the simple answer of those who are ignorant and mentally lazy. But man felt helpless and had need of gods who would protect him from natural calamities.

FRANCIS BACON

This bold and original thinker was concerned with man. He wanted man to make proper use of his mind, and thus to widen his horizon. He felt that human thinking should draw upon nature in forming its conclusions, for nature is an inexhaustible source of true knowledge.

Before beginning his exploration, however, man should clear his mind of any preconceived ideas. Only in this way will he be a true pioneer in the search for truth. Then whatever he discovers will be his own achievement and a genuine contribution.

In his most fundamental work, *Novum Organum,* Bacon makes this statement: "The very contemplation of things as they are, without superstition or imposture, error or confusion, is in itself more worthy than all the fruit of invention. His purpose, he adds, is "to try whether I cannot in very fact lay more firmly the foundations, and extend more widely the limits, of man's power and greatness."[9]

Thus preoccupied with man's grandeur, he refrained from speculation about the existence or nonexistence of God. In fact, he forbade himself any doubt about the Author of all things. "Everything has its beginning in God," he affirms. He rejects atheism as a superficial philosophy. "I had rather believe all the fables in The Legend, and the Talmud and the Alcoran, than that this universal frame is without a mind . . . a little philosophy inclines man's mind to atheism; but depth in philosophy bringeth man's mind back to religion. For while the mind of man looketh upon the second causes scattered, it may sometimes rest in them and go no further; but when it beholdeth the chain of them, confederate and linked together, it must needs fly to Providence and Deity."[10]

Bacon does not challenge the mysteries of creation, but he severely castigates all attempts to mix theology with philosophy. "The corruption of philosophy by superstition and an admixture of theology is far more widely spread, and does the greatest harm, whether to entire systems or to their parts."

The admixture of religion with philosophy, or, for that matter, with science, involves starting with premises which are held to be unquestionable, about first and last causes. Thus it preempts, as it were, any further speculation one might venture.

"It is the very plague of the understanding for vanity to become an object of veneration. Yet some of the moderns have with extreme levity indulged in this vanity to the extent of attempting to base a system of natural philosophy on the first chapter of Genesis, on the Book of Job, and other parts of the sacred writings."[11]

People who attempt to establish a system based on religious beliefs are the ones most likely to attack the discoveries of science as profane and a danger to religious faith. "Neither is it to be forgotten that in every age natural philosophy has had adversaries who are troublesome and hard to deal with, namely superstition and the blind and immoderate zeal of religion. Even in ancient Greece, some of those who pointed to natural causes as an explanation for natural phenomena were accused of impiety." And he adds: "Nor was much more forebearance shown by some ancient fathers of the Christian church toward those who maintained, on most convincing grounds (such as no one would now dream of contradicting), that the earth was round and that consequently the antipodes existed.[12] In this last sentence, Bacon is referring to Copernicus and Galileo.

Bacon's remarks could very well be cited today as evidence of the permanent feud which exists between natural scientists and the advocates of religion, who view the efforts of these researchers as a menace to their domination of simple souls. As Bacon says, trying to mix the human with the divine is degrading to both.[13]

PASCAL

He was a scientist of the first order as well as an inventor, whose genius was apparent at an early age. But science led him from labyrinth to labyrinth; it could never satisfy his unquenchable thirst for absolute truth. Finally he gave it up in desperation and joined the rigid order of the Jansenists. He then launched vitriolic attacks against the Jesuits because he thought they were too lenient in their interpretation of sin and the dogmas. He would admit of no compromise.

His fiery soul so yearned for transcendence that it literally consumed his body. God was revealed to him in nature when he observed that the design of the infinitely vast and the very minute were identical, both being part of the same noble and constructive plan. The spectacle of the universe filled him with awe and made man seem utterly insignificant. He felt that he was terribly small and weak. But his next thought was that man occupies a very special place in nature's plan. He realized that this weak creature was endowed with a superior intelligence which had made it ruler of the planet. "Man is a feeble reed, but a thinking reed." Thus does Pascal exalt human intelligence, yet he repudiates it whenever it interferes with his faith.

Pascal, who is a visionary and a poet as well as a scientist, constantly grapples with contradictory conclusions about God and nature, about the immortality of the soul: "This is what I see and what troubles me. Searching on all sides, I find only darkness everywhere. Nature presents me with nothing which is not a subject of doubt and concern. If I saw nothing there which revealed a divinity, I would come to a negative conclusion; if I saw everywhere the signs of a Creator, I would remain peacefully in the faith. But seeing too much to deny and too little to be sure, I am in a state to be pitied; wherefore I have a hundred times wished that if a God maintains nature, she should testify to Him unequivocally, and that if the signs she gives are deceptive, she should suppress them altogether; that she should say everything or nothing, that I might see what causes I have to follow. Whereas in my present state, ignorant of what I am or what I ought to do, I know neither my condition nor my duty. My heart inclines wholly to know in what direction the true good lies, in order to follow it. For me, no price could be too high for eternity."[14]

The above quotation exemplifies Pascal's mental torment. "Seeing too much to deny and too little to be sure" presents in a nutshell the dilemma of every thinking person. "Thought constitutes the greatness of man," he notes further. It is not merely a question of knowing but also of knowing that he is capable of knowing. If man concludes that he can never penetrate the unknown, man is degraded. Pascal was never able to rid himself of doubt. For him, God remained eternally hidden, though he had sought Him with all his heart.

Oscillating between positivistic materialism and complete surrender to the faith, he finally chooses the latter and takes refuge in Christianity. He justifies his decision in these words: "The heart has its reasons, which reason knows not of."[15] And having chosen, he has to resort to reason to justify his choice. He argues that Christianity is superior because it is the only religion which can make man humble and proud at the same time—humble because it teaches man that he is subject to misery and corruption; proud because he knows that he can attain a more perfect state through the gospels and divine grace. Pascal points out that Christianity is the only religion which teaches that faith is a gift of God. Others appeal only to man's reason to prove God exists.

Pascal's *Thoughts* is the only piece of writing left to us which can shed any light upon his inner life. It reveals an extraordinary man, full of doubt but reaching out for God. He knows that he is lost and cries out for help, unlike many others who never thought to question but just accept what they are told. What faith he has he attributes to God's grace, and he struggles to believe more wholeheartedly and to profess that he believes. But Pascal, though he ardently desired to convince others, could never quite convince himself. Thus he could never be, as he puts it, "at peace in the faith." He was unable to shed all doubt and rise to the crystalline purity of total faith. Such faith does not need to assert itself. Pascal's continual vacillation between faith and reason turned him into a religious fanatic. Fanaticism helped him to assuage his doubts and silence the devil's advocate, whose voice distracted him during his fervent prayers.

SPINOZA

No two philosophers could be more different from one another than Spinoza and Pascal. Spinoza did not fight publicly for his convictions, but preferred a quiet retreat where he could devote himself to the understanding of God's nature. In spite of this preoccupation with God, he did not take refuge in religion. He remained at a distance because he found that all religions were anthropocentric, that is, they were concerned only with God's relation to man. In Spinoza's view, man was only one of the innumerable manifestations of the creative spirit.

God, says Spinoza, is all spirit and all substance. His are the eternal laws that rule the Cosmos. They govern all movement, every single action in the universe. And so on earth the plants, and animals, including man, act as God conditioned them to, according to their inherent nature. Everything that happens has a cause, and that cause itself is the effect of a prior cause, and so on, until we finally get back to God. But Spinoza's first cause differs from Plato's and Aristotle's Prime Mover in this respect: God Himself is subject to his own eternal laws. "God is indwelling and not the transient cause of things," he says in *Ethics*.[16]

This idea that all matter is animated by His spirit originated with Giordano Bruno, and for this theory he was burnt at the stake. Therefore, Spinoza was careful not to voice this belief publicly, even though Holland was thought to be a tolerant country. He believed that not only man, but all things have a soul; that soul is the emanation of the Universal Spirit which is God's essence. All that exists has a double nature: matter and spirit. Matter is but the manifestation of the Universal Spirit.

To say that everything which exists is moved by the same universal spirit to which God Himself is subject, is very close to saying that God is the same as the universe, a purely pantheistic statement. The spirit which animates all things is never at rest; it is the antithesis of death, for death, as we conceive it, is matter at rest or in decomposition. The universal spirit uses matter, either living, or in transition to a new form or mode, in order to recreate life. Creation is a never-ending process.

The German poet, Goethe, expresses the same thought in this verse taken from *Faust:*

In flood of life, in action's storm
I ply my wave
with waving motion
Birth and the grave,
a boundless ocean,
ceaselessly giving
weft of living,

forms unending,
glowing and blending
So work I on the whirring forms of time,
The life that clothes the deity sublime.[17]

Since God is bound by His own law, He cannot change anything, nor can he wish to do so. If it were otherwise, Spinoza
explains, it would mean that something had been missing before; that God or the Universe had been imperfect. Spinoza,
like Seneca, scoffs at those who think they can persuade God
to grant their wishes by promising something or making a vow.
Such people are ignorant of God's nature; they believe God
exists for man's benefit. An anthropocentric view of the universe postulates a universe in which everything, including God,
is bound to serve man, a view which somewhat degrades God.

Spinoza maintains that the language of the Bible is deliberately metaphorical or allegorical because it was intended to
attract the multitudes. "The Scriptures were written primarily
for an entire people, and secondarily for the whole human race;
therefore, its contents must necessarily be adapted, as far as
possible, to the understanding of the masses." People need
miracles in order to believe, and the Bible offers them abundantly. Miracles are phenomena that are beyond people's understanding, and so inspire awe. Any literal interpretation of
the Bible shows it to be full of errors, contradictions, and obvious impossibilities.

One suspects that Spinoza did not dare to attack the Bible
openly because it was believed to be based on revelation, though
many parts of it are an insult to human reason. He rejects the
dogmas, regardless of their source; he does not believe in the
divinity of Jesus, but reveres him as "the greatest and noblest
of the prophets." "The eternal wisdom of God has shown itself
in all things, but chiefly in the mind of man, and most of all
in Jesus Christ."

Spinoza's doctrine implies that human intelligence, though
it is part of the Universal Mind, fades with the death of the
body. Individual man is like an arrow which is sent out to

complete its trajectory, and then merges with collective immortality. This doctrine holds out no salvation, no heavenly bliss. But it does away with hell also, and the fear of everlasting torment. It is a positive doctrine, in that it emphasizes man's ability to rise above the mixture of good and evil in his nature in striving for the perfection of an ideal. His view of man is close to that of the Stoics, who held that true virtue seeks no reward for doing good. Spinoza's followers will find their reward in the serenity and contentment that comes with constructive activity.

Many will reject his philosophy because it leaves out transcendence; nor does it allow for divine grace in human life. Arnauld, who was head of the Jansenists, called Spinoza "the most impious and most dangerous man of his age."

Others, however, will find inspiration in the simplicity and grandeur of his doctrine. His view of God and the Cosmos, his belief in man's capacity for virtue and idealism, had great appeal during his lifetime, and his influence is still evident today.[18]

DESCARTES

The father of modern science, who deduced that he existed because he could think, applied this same criterion in proving God's reality. "The existence of God is much more evident than that of any sensible thing."

Yet man is incapable of forming any clear idea of God. "All the knowledge that we can have of God in this life, barring miracles, derives from reasoning and from the sequence of our words that are based on principles of faith which is obcure or comes from natural ideas and notions within us. And these ideas, however clear they may seem, can only be clumsy and obscure in dealing with such an exalted subject."

God can only be imagined as the embodiment of perfection. "The substance which we understand to be supremely perfect and in which we conceive nothing which comprises any fault, or limitation upon perfection, is called God." "The most perfect thing that we can conceive: this is what all men call God." God's very essence is perfection. "Knowing that he is the most perfect being, to whom all the absolute perfections belong, I ought not to attribute to him anything that I have not recognized to be absolutely perfect; and everything that I can so imagine and conceive to be absolutely perfect, simply from the fact that I can imagine it, belongs to the nature of God."

The above quotations imply that God is perfect but that His creatures are not. Certainly, we can think of nothing in our human world that is absolutely perfect. God's creatures can be improved and are in need of improvement, whereas He is that Being which is "immutable, all-knowing, all powerful, infinite, eternal, free, and by whom I, myself, and all other things which exist (if it is true that any other things do exist) have been created."

The attributes of God which Descartes arrived at by means of meditation are essentially the same as those which the Scholastic philosophers used to define Him. And thinking of God, the scientist in Descartes needed no confirmation. No miracle was required to convince him of God's reality. Yet he would not deny the validity of miracles, should God choose to perform one.

"One ought not to say there is anything that God cannot do; given that every species of truth and goodness depends upon his omnipotence, I would not even say that God could not make a mountain without a valley, or rule that one and two would not make three." This emphatic statement concerning God's omnipotence is found in a letter which Descartes wrote to Arnauld, who was leader of the Jansenists, a fundamentalist sect. Yet in spite of this avowal, the Jansenists and the Church authorities as well doubted Descartes' sincerity. They suspected him of being a heretic or even an atheist, because he had deliberately rejected the Book of Genesis and many other parts of the Bible. His language in doing so was cautious but nevertheless forceful. "Anyone who can explain (the book of Genesis to me), or the Song of Solomon, or the Book of Revelation, would seem to me to be a veritable Apollo." And again: "As for the Book of Genesis, the story of creation given there is perhaps metaphorical; it ought therefore to be left to the theologians. And the creation need not be taken as divided into six days; rather, the division should be made according to our manner of conceiving it. St. Augustine gives us an example of this in his *Thoughts on the Angels*."[19]

The scientist in Descartes revolts against the biblical account of separation of light from darkness: "When Genesis says that God separated the light from darkness, it means that he separated the good angels from the evil ones. One cannot actually separate a privation from a positive quality, and it is for this reason that the text cannot be taken literally."[20]

Meditating on God in human terms, within the limitations of human thinking, Descartes himself is baffled and gets into difficulty. "Who created God?" he asks himself. All answer to this question can only be a non-answer. He continues, "Although God has always existed, nevertheless, because he actually conserves himself, it is quite proper to call him the cause of himself."[21]

The church understood that Descartes, the embodiment of doubt, represented a danger to its doctrine. It called him godless, heretic; it harassed him and prevented him from teaching at a university in Holland. His works were publicly burned. He let himself be persuaded by the Queen of Sweden to move to her country, where in 1650, he succumbed to the rigor of the climate.

KANT

Kant was one of the most powerful of the philosophers and can be said to have influenced all those who came after him.

He was led to reject reason, the usual recourse of the philosophers, in his attempt to understand God. In his monumental work, *The Critique of Pure Reason,* he struggled for hundreds of pages, only to conclude that reason was inadequate in this regard, that only faith and instinct can help man. Such a statement might have come from someone who had decided, as Pascal did, to reject science in favor of religion, and dedicate his life to God. Kant, however, did not do this. The "Sage of Königsberg" simply separated these two things in his mind. One compartment was for worldly knowledge, another was for feeling.

Kant asserted that our feeling that God exists is innate, *à priori,* that is, prior to intellectual development. The feeling that God exists is the source of our morality, and it makes man unique. It is this moral sense that guides us throughout our lives; it is the source of our belief in a life after the death of the body.

"Belief in God and in another world are so interwoven with my moral sentiment that, as there is little danger of my losing the latter, there is also little cause to fear that the former can be taken from me."[22]

Kant rejects the argument from design, namely, that nature's perfection demonstrates the existence of the Creator, for actually, there is a great deal of chaos and disorder in nature. He also takes issue with the ontological argument—that knowledge of God is intuitive and immediate; yet he uses the same argument to explain morality. This moral perception leads us to God, to the perception of God.

Kant emphatically rejected the notion that God is a myth, simply because there is no way to demonstrate his existence. "From what source could we, through purely speculative employment of reason, derive the knowledge that there is no Supreme Being as the ultimate goal of all things?" he asks. Atheism is at least as presumptuous as religious faith. To Kant God was an inaccessible ideal in the mind of man, a concept without blemish, complete, and the crown of human knowledge.

When all is said and done, Kant's faith was as simple and uncomplicated as that of the simplest churchgoer who totally lacks education. The belief in God supported him in his life, but it did not prevent him from castigating the priests who used religion to control men's minds. He always approved of the French Revolution.

LEIBNIZ

Leibniz, who was born a good twenty years after Pascal, was one of the most brilliant and most original philosophers to appear in the latter part of the seventeenth century. He was certain that there must be a Creator. Like Pascal, he arrived at this conviction through the contemplation of the Universe, both the macrocosm and the microcosm—that is, the great and the little world. The latter was revealed to him through the microscope, a new and truly marvelous invention of that day. Leibniz, like Pascal before him, was filled with awe and wonder at the spectacle. But he did not reject reason, as Pascal had done, in trying to explain the phenomenon.

Leibniz stated the first principle of his philosophy thus: the minute, or invisible world is an exact replica of the great world, having the same organization, the same plan. Moreover—and this is the most important part of his theory on the Universe—he declared that each segment also constitutes an exact replica of the whole, and each segment of that segment does the same. The Universe is a wondrous machine in which each cog constitutes an independent machine functioning within the larger framework. Together they form the system of a vast universe, composed of countless smaller universes; or, if one prefers, each part of the world machine is itself a machine. To Leibniz, the magic of reality was almost unbelievable. Discovering its secrets offers the greatest challenge man has yet encountered.

Leibniz undertook to meet this challenge, to explain the

Universe on entirely rational grounds. The Universe of universes is the way it is, he says, because every part of it is moved by the same driving force, the Substance which emanates from God, who is the prime, or the supreme reality. This moving force, or Substance, this Creative Intelligence, which the Greeks called "Noús," infuses all things. The Spirit, or Noús, sometimes called Substance or Soul, is the reality, says Leibniz. Matter is but the representation, or rather the manifestation, of the Spirit. It is therefore inherently imperfect.

Leibniz calls the units that constitute the Universe Monads, a designation that connotes individuality or uniqueness. God is the Supreme Monad, the Perfect Being who is eternally himself. The universe changes, God does not. He is eternal.

The fact that every part of His great work fits into the whole, yet constitutes a clockwork on its own, reveals a grandiose design, which Leibniz calls the Pre-established Harmony. The Nous penetrates everything so that the whole universe throbs with life, striving continually to satisfy the inherent Thought. Decaying matter also lives, though on a different plane. For Leibniz there is no death in the universe.

> A world of creatures, living beings, animals, entelechies and souls, exist in the minutest part of matter. Each portion of matter may be conceived as a garden full of plants, or a pond full of fish. But every stem of a plant, every limb of an animal, every drop of sap or blood is also such a garden or pond. And though the ground and air interspersed between the plants of the garden, or the water interspersed between the fish of the pond, may not themselves be pond or fish, yet they contain them. Thus there is nothing arid, sterile, or dead in the universe, no chaos, or confusion, save in appearance; exactly as a pond would appear to us at a distance were we able to see only the confused movement of the swarming fish and not the fish themselves.[23]

In spite of their individuality, it is obvious that each monad has meaning only in relation to the others. Each individual part of the universe is endowed with part of the Nous, it stands on its own and is important in itself, but only within the framework of the Plan. Individualism is concomitant with a planned function, a planned destiny. And God has foreseen this contradiction per se, this freedom within determinism, the synthesis of antithetic forces, for God is omniscient.

Omniscience is one of the three qualities Leibniz attributes to the Supreme Being, the other two being omnipotence and benevolence. The Author of the Supreme Plan must indeed be all-powerful to enforce the laws which maintain the universe in eternal harmony despite the constant strife of its components. God, being omniscient, foresaw the clash of contradictory forces; he must have willed them to conform to the plan. Life and destruction, decay and regeneration have meaning only to us; they represent the unfolding of the timeless adventure of creation. Leibniz felt that God, the perfect being, must have wanted this world as it is, with all its contradictions, for this universe was His creation and he viewed it with benevolence. Such as it is, it must be the best possible world, worthy of the Wisest, Most Powerful, and Most Benevolent One.

God preordains everything, and thus each of us forms a part of God's essence. God differs from man in Degree only. Man is endowed with a greater share of the universal Nous than any other creature on the planet. This enables him to grasp more of the Universal Plan, more of God's wisdom. For Leibniz, knowledge is not just the understanding of a given subject but enlightenment. True knowledge strives to advance on the road that leads to the Divine. The more we search for this kind of knowledge, the more we use our Scientific advances to gain this kind of understanding, the higher we will stand in the universe. The further we extend our exploration, and the more we develop our potential, the more enlightened we shall become—and the more liberated, according to Leibniz—for he equates enlightenment with inner freedom. This is a simple thought but significant, for it contains Kant's moral imperative and is also the basis for twentieth century existentialism. He who does not develop his potential remains only a statistic.

One is reminded of Ibsen's condemnation of Peer Gynt: "You

were neither deliberately good nor deliberately evil; you will be recast in the Button-Molder's ladle, as waste material—to be recycled."

Leibniz criticized his great contemporary, Spinoza, saying:

> Although Spinoza occasionally has beautiful thoughts, which are by no means abhorrent, as I have shown, nevertheless, his main doctrines are not capable of the least proof, and in fact, are not proved by him despite his claim to have given the demonstration. For him there is only one substance, and this is God. Creatures he regards as modes or affections of God. God is without understanding and will, does not act according to final causes, but by a necessity of his nature, just as the properties of the circle follow from its essence. He believes, indeed, that our mind will survive death, but it will no longer perceive the present, future, nor remember the past. All happiness, stripped of its precious wrappings, comes to this, that recognizing the inevitability of things, we should be content to accept them as they come. Is not the Christian view better and truer?[24]

In spite of this criticism, there are no essential differences between his and Spinoza's philosophy. For both, matter is animated by God's substance, the creative intelligence of the universe. Spinoza says that all things have properties conditioned by God; Leibniz professes that God has made the universe function according to a pre-established harmony. Spinoza, like Leibniz, identifies nature with God. Leibniz amplified this thought by saying that all parts of matter represent the plan of the whole universe, that each unit comprises the entire plan down to the minutest details. Both philosophers see the universe as unity within diversity (diversity within unity?). Leibniz criticizes Spinoza's doctrine that there is no personal survival, that the intelligence housed in the brain will return, after death, to the great pool of the universe, and individual identity will be annihilated. He argues that such a doctrine deprives humans of all incentive to do good. He recognizes that the Stoics preached that virtue is its own reward, but says that the beneficial consequences of one's good deeds cannot inspire a person if they occur after his death. Leibniz has a narrow view about virtue, not recognizing its redeeming value for mankind. He asserts that the purpose of knowledge is to increase virtue.

Reason for Leibniz is the instrument of morality. Rational thinking should persuade the human race to practice virtue. He envisions the creation on earth of a City of God, which he calls "the truly universal monarchy." It is for him the consummation of rational activity, the true purpose, the ultimate reason for human existence. Each of us can gain citizenship in the City of God by using our reason, which will lead us to establish a harmonious world here below, similar to the system we observe in the universe. To accomplish this would be the highest achievement. To acknowledge that someone contributed to this goal is the highest praise possible.

Voltaire, in his pamphlet, *Candide,* scoffed at Leibniz' assertion that this is the best possible world. The hero of this tale is the victim of, and witness to, human stupidity, the innocent dupe of hypocrisy, greed and intolerance in others. Leibniz wanted to demonstrate that, though individuals are fallible, human actions are powerless to interfere with universal harmony. As Leibniz says, humans, like other creatures, are but "the fulgurations of divinity from moment to moment, limited by the imperfect receptivity which is inherent in their nature." Voltaire's satire was unfair because it attempted to reduce the metaphysics of Leibniz to the human plane.

VOLTAIRE

His very name arouses passions to this day. It is the symbol of natural religion, of the fight against superstition and ignorance, and also of the fight of an individual against the power of the Church over the masses.

Voltaire was called an atheist and worse; but those who knew him maintained that he spoke of the Supreme Being with reverence and awe. In fact, his ire was directed against the "cruel priests and their tyrannical God." He was referring to authorities of the Christian Church and particularly those of the Catholic Church, who threatened people with excommunication, hell and damnation, and subjected them to every sort of harassment in order to maintain their hold on them.

For much of his life, Voltaire was considered flippant. Though he covered Church and State with sarcasm, he was tolerated because he was a member of high society and was not taken seriously, or thought to be a threat to the establishment. Then came the infamous Callas affair, which was mentioned in a previous chapter. Deeply shaken by this obvious manifestation of religious fanaticism, Voltaire was revolted by such intolerance and injustice. He dedicated his life from then on to fighting bigotry. He coined this motto: "Ecrasons l'infâme!"—"Let us crush the Infamous!"—meaning the Roman Church. He used this motto at the end of all his letters and notes, as a reminder to himself and others.

Voltaire's religion is a simple one. Though aware of the existence of a Creator, he professed that we, his creatures, are incapable of really knowing anything about him, and those who pretend to interpret his will are impostors. Man, practicing the good, is doing God's work. Voltaire was troubled all his life by the problem of evil and could not understand why God should tolerate it. He was never able to find an answer that satisfied him. This question has been debated throughout history, and basically, the answers boil down to this: He cannot or will not prevent evil on this earth.

Deeply troubled by what he saw and experienced around him, Voltaire resented Leibniz' assumption that this was the best of all possible worlds. Voltaire's answer to this point of view, set forth in *Candide,* was that certain calamities besetting man are caused by nature, but most of man's troubles are brought on chiefly by man himself. This piece of writing about a foolish and bumbling optimist proved to be a masterpiece which is still widely read and appreciated to this day.

Voltaire rejected atheism, for he was sure that the universe had a Creator, though man could not know Him. To say that God does not exist is just as presumptuous, according to Voltaire, as to believe in revelations. Moreover, the logic of his natural religion forced him to deny the divinity of Jesus, and most emphatically, the resurrection of the body. He is supposed to have said, "I am not a Christian because I want to love God better." He did not feel bound by the tenets of Christian religions, and felt free to adore, but not to worship God. His natural religion also taught him that all is temporal and that the world is renewed in eternal cycles; as a scientist, he took a dim view of the doctrine of the survival of the soul after death.

> Nobody thinks of giving an immortal soul to a flea; why then to an elephant, or a monkey, or my valet? . . . A child dies in its mother's womb, just at the moment when it has received a soul. Will it rise again fetus, or boy, or man? To rise again—to be the same person that you were—you must have your memory perfectly fresh and present, for it is memory that makes your identity. If your memory be lost, how will you be the same man? . . . Why do mankind flatter themselves that they are gifted with a spiritual and immortal principle? . . . Perhaps from their inordinate vanity. I am persuaded that if a peacock could speak, he would boast of his soul, and would affirm that it inhabited his magnificent tail.[25]

In earlier times, Voltaire could never have gotten away with his daring attacks on the clergy and religious dogma. But he lived in a somewhat more enlightened age and was, as it were, a spokesman for his contemporaries; he gave voice to ideas which had germinated in the minds of many. Nevertheless, he was subjected to a considerable amount of harassment and persecution from the authorities; he eluded them by living in a house on the border of France and Switzerland so he could slip to the other side if they were after him.

Voltaire's reputation as a defender of the oppressed, a champion of tolerance and a father to the people grew incessantly. He was considered the prophet of his nation, a leader, in contradistinction to the ruling dynasty and to the Church. His return to Paris in 1778 was a triumph such as had been given only to emperors, but more spontaneous. Yet the priest who heard his final confession refused to give him absolution unless he would sign a confession of full faith in the Catholic doctrine. On February 28, 1778, Voltaire then drew up a statement: "I die adoring God, loving my friends, not hating my enemies, and detesting superstition."

The Church execrated his memory, but his influence on the thinking of his contemporaries was profound. One can state without exaggeration that the establishment of the cult of the Supreme Being, shortly after his death, was inspired by his natural religion.

The Church had been shaken up by Voltaire's attacks. A priest called Père Lacordaire is supposed to have made this astonishing statement: "God, with devilish cunning, (sic) sent Voltaire to combat the Church in order to regenerate it."

HEGEL

Every thesis is opposed by an antithesis and, in nature's plan, all opposites unite in a synthesis. This is the gist of Hegel's view, the Theory of the Universal Plan.

God is the Absolute Principle, in whom all conflicts are resolved. Good and evil become neutralized in Him. Evil may serve good, as, for example, death serves life. The rational universe is a composite of diversities.

Hegel's postulate resolves the age-old enigma as to why God tolerates evil. One might very well wonder why death annihilates the most illustrious minds, and why all life must be extinguished. He sees life and death as the two poles of eternal renewal.

God's realm is the invisible Church. In his youth Hegel rebelled against the established Christian churches, declaring: "Religion and politics joined forces (or: were bedfellows); religion taught what despotism wanted it to teach, that is, contempt for mankind. It denied man's ability to produce anything good through his own efforts."

At that stage of his life, Hegel also maintained that the Christian community was not the community of God because from its inception it was based on "church discipline and Christian police institutions." He dreamed of a popular religion imbued with the spirit of unity and functioning without coercion—a religion of reason. He saw that harmony on earth is not a gift of God; it must be established by virtuous men. Hegel and the two closest friends of his youth, Hölderlin the poet, and Schelling the philosopher, created this motto for themselves: "God's realm is coming and our hands should not be idle in our laps." God is pure reason, which is unbounded. The very word "spirit" implies the absence of limitations. Therefore, He cannot be encompassed by any church or state.

Faith in God's realm is faith in mankind, faith in one's self. Christianity is the faith of one segment of mankind, but it can never establish God's realm on earth because it cannot close the gap between its Absolute God and helpless man.

Hegel's religious community was to be inspired by a common language, common customs, imbued with virtue and piety. In this ideal community religion would play a fundamental role, but restrict itself to making people conscious that man's nature is identical with God's. This, rather than any particular doctrine, should inspire religious life. In such a community, religion and state would form a synthesis; religion would become philosophy.[26]

Later in life, Hegel found such an ideal merger of religious and human freedom in the Prussian state. He declared that the freedom of Protestantism is not incompatible with the state.

Hegel's philosophical journey began with rebellion against church and state, yet wound up extolling both. In his philosophical peregrinations as well as in his personal career, he managed to unite opposites merging thesis and antithesis to reach a synthesis, a satisfactory compromise. No wonder that later his followers, the neo-Hegelians, drew opposite conclusions from his teachings; some hailed him as the forerunner of Marx, while others insisted on his orthodoxy.

The German nation greatly admired Hegel and recognized him as one of their great. His birthday fell one day after Goethe's; both were celebrated together. In fact, there are many elements in Hegel's ambiguous philosophy that Germans could identify with. Not only Germans of his own day, but those who followed Hitler, found in it some of their basic beliefs. His idea of a "Volksreligion," a community religion, as opposed to a Christian community, and his virulent anti-semitism were to constitute the cornerstone of Hitler's national socialistic state.[27]

EINSTEIN

The road to God opens for man when he becomes aware of the mystery that envelops the universe. Without this sense of mystery, says Einstein, men would be no different from the other creatures. There is something mysterious about all creative activity. The artist, the scientist, the poet, and the philosopher all strive to express their exultation or their awe "in a humble attitude before the grandeur of reason, incarnate in existence and which, in its profoundest depths, is inaccessible to man."

Equating religious feeling with this sense of mystery about creation, Einstein rejects organized, anthropomorphic religion as practiced by the churches and adopted by the great majority of people. A personal God, he explains, was created in man's image by those who feared the unknown or wanted to exploit people's fear of it. The concept of an anthropomorphic god, of a God reduced to human proportions, placed vast power in the hands of priests. They claimed to be intermediaries between men and God; the power to bless or to curse was vested in them.

The concept of an anthropomorphic God was, and still is, a source of conflict between religion and science. Those who adhere to this concept reject the discoveries of science; they fear

96

that to accept them would put an end to their personal privileges.

An ideal religion should appeal to what is good, beautiful, and true in humanity itself. "In their struggle for the ethical good, teachers of religion must have the stature to give up the notion of a personal God, that is, give up that source of fear and hope which in the past placed such vast power in the hands of priests."

The Church is useful to the extent that it fosters the concept of universal mystery; the task of science is to try to solve the unsolved that surrounds us. In this respect science and religion can and should collaborate, for the common good.

Einstein maintained that religious feeling, far from being alien to the scientist, is actually his distinguishing characteristic. A true scientist is always imbued with religious *feeling*. The word "feeling" must be emphasized in Einstein's concept, because, for him, true religiosity has nothing to do with doctrines. He feels the divine everywhere at work in the universe. This way of thinking brings Einstein very close to Spinoza, who was obviously an inspiration to him. Any scientific endeavor, properly conceived, is a religious act. "Science without religion is lame," but he adds, "religion without science is blind."[28]

Einstein's "cosmic religion" has nothing to do with the notion of hell or heaven. He does not believe in the survival of the individual soul, a concept that, in his opinion, has been invented by the priests to inspire fear or hope in their followers and thus to dominate them.

"I cannot imagine a God who rewards and punishes the objects of his creation, whose purposes are modeled after our own—a God, in short, who is but a reflection of human frailty. Neither can I believe that the individual survives the death of his body, although feeble souls harbor this belief through fear or ridiculous egotism. It is enough for me to contemplate the mystery of conscious life through all eternity."[29]

Science purifies man, removing the dross of personal desire.

True science is religious; it unites people in selfless labor. If man develops his talents in order to help others, he is serving the universal design. A religious person is one who directs his thoughts toward superpersonal values—one whose aspirations transcend his own personal comfort and well-being.

Ethics were the basis of Einstein's religion. In this he resembles Kant and Spinoza. Einstein, however, believed that the foundations of morality were best embodied in the Judeo-Christian religion.

Following Einstein's train of thought, we discover a God whose omnipotence sustains his creation and whose infinite wisdom manifests itself in nature. Communication with the Divine will not be established by prayer, but by dedication to the service of mankind (Einstein emphatically insists on this), and through efforts to learn as much as possible about the cosmic design. The task of religion should be to help people in these efforts, to point out the oneness of the creature with his Creator and with all creation.

SCHOPENHAUER

The author of *The World as Will and Idea* shows little preoccupation with God or with man's relation to God. For him, it is the will that is the life-generating force; it is the will, the inner drive, the iner fire or passion, that moves human actions. Usually the will dominates the intellect, subordinates it, uses it for its own purposes. One does things because one wants to do them, and afterwards finds reasons for having done them.

The will, this primordial, savage force, can, however, be tamed by the intellect. Religion acts as a "quieter" of the will. God, who judges human actions, opposes the unbridled will. Religion is capable of divining the motives behind these actions and classifying them as delusive and transitory. He who can see the world in this light has reached a state of grace. The more complete this state, the closer man has come to achieving what Schopenhauer regards as his "salvation." His definition of this word is somewhat different from the Christian one. To Schopenhauer, salvation means renunciation of life's desires. The more man tries to rise above earthly contingencies, the closer he comes to a state of perfect bliss. This is so, Schopenhauer says, because life is suffering.

The original sin, as set forth in the Bible, was the sin of engendering life, thereby causing strife and suffering. "We found, however, that suffering is essential to life as a whole, and inseparable from it. Every wish proceeds from a need, from a want, or from a suffering; every satisfaction is therefore but the removal of the pain, and brings no positive happiness. The joys deceive us, presenting themselves as a positive good, but in truth they have only a negative nature, and are only the end of the evil."[30]

Since life is a state of suffering, nonbeing appears to Schopenhauer as the only true state of bliss. He judges the various religions from this point of view, namely, whether they affirm or deny the value of human existence. The Greeks rank the lowest because Greek mythology extolls life. Judaism is better, but still too optimistic, in his judgment. Christianity comes closer to his ideal; in his view, the story of Calvary and the crucifixion of Jesus symbolize the denial of life. "Certainly the doctrine of original sin (assertion of the will) and of salvation (denial of the will) is the central idea of Christianity; what remains are only the vestments and outer trappings. Jesus Christ should therefore be regarded as the universal symbol of personification of the denial of life and never as an individual; whether it is the mythical character portrayed in the Gospels or the real man whose history is probably the basis of the Biblical accounts."[31]

Schopenhauer sees Buddhism as the most perfect religion; the bliss of Nirvana, a pure state of nonbeing which necessitates no rebirth, is more in keeping with his own philosophy. Individuals may ascend from lower to higher states of consciousness as they gradually atone for original sin.

Schopenhauer's somber philosophy deals a severe blow to the concept of a benevolent God, a loving father who listens to our prayers and forgives our sins if we repent of them. God is nowhere, or in any case, obscure. Good and evil may be judged by accepted human standards, but life itself is evil, atonement for a sin committed by someone whose soul now haunts another individual. Actually, man's only option is to renounce all desires, thus cleansing himself of the impurity of existence. And somewhere in the offing is a Judge who decides when the individual deserves Nirvana. What the latter state consists of will never be revealed to man; he only knows that it will liberate him from the punishment of rebirth. Will the creature who has attained Nirvana be dissolved in the great pool of Spirit? What will be its final destiny? Schopenhauer ignores such questions. He does not concern himself with theology.

BERGSON

Bergson's approach to God is through evolution. His point of departure is life itself, life being a dynamic force, which he calls "élan vital," that is a twin brother to Schopenhauer's "will." This driving force cannot, by its very nature, remain static; it must create. Creation means experimentation with ever new varieties of animals, plants, and cosmic bodies. Creation is renewal. Varieties of a given species are not merely the result of natural selection, as Darwin stated, nor are they the result of outside forces; they are the outcome of an instinct or impetus that is within them.

As varieties develop from a common source, their differences will become more distinct. Nature proceeds by disassociation and by duplication. Let us consider, for example, the idea of the eye. The eye is enormously complex, yet its function is simple, which is a continual source of wonder to us.

The very word "evolution" implied motion. The word "élan" (impetus) means creation. "The impetus of which we speak consists briefly of an exigency of creation. This is true of every manifestation of life. Nothing worthwhile can be brought forth without an inner drive. Art will not be original, but at best imitative. A scientist who does not have this drive but just skill and routine will not achieve a breakthrough, though he might make chance discoveries."[32]

Bergson's view of evolution as the result of the creative drive that permeates the universe is the key to his religious belief. He rejects out of hand all religion that is based on tradition and ritual. Such religion is static; it lacks the dynamic force which is the essence of true religion. Religion should recognize the greatness and beauty of creation; should express and interpret its meaning.

"The spectacle of what religions have been in the past, of what certain religions still are today, is indeed a disgrace to human intelligence. What error and folly! Experience may say, 'that is false,' and reason, 'that is absurd.' Humanity clings all the more to that absurdity and that error." And if this were all! But religion has even been known to enjoin immorality, to prescribe crime. "The cruder it is, the more actual space it occupies in the life of a people. What it will have to share later with science, art, and philosophy, it demands and obtains at first for itself alone. And that is indeed a matter for surprise, seeing that we began by defining man as an intelligent being. We find societies with neither science, art, nor philosophy, but there has never been one without religion."[33]

And Bergson continues: "Animals are, as far as we know, incapable of religious sense. *Homo sapiens* is the only creature endowed with reason; he is also the only creature to pin its existence to things unreasonable."[34]

No philosopher spoke out more boldly against church, against organized religion, than Bergson. He sees the origin of religion as a reaction to the realization that death is inevitable. Knowing that he must die, man consoles himself with the belief that he will live in spirit after his death. The dead continued, in primitive societies, to be members of those societies. They were believed to know more about universal mysteries than the living. This gave rise to ancestor worship and superstition, and ancestor worship led to the creation of gods.

To accept or reject a religion one must examine what is really religious in it. One cannot pass from static religion to dynamic religion through enlargement or improvement. Static religion is mere compliance with ritual; dynamic religion makes people love and follow what is good.

The creative impulse that presides over creation is what men used to call God. God is life that never ceases to evolve. God is not a person, but a force. He is cosmic intelligence. The creature, as soon as created, is free, and in turn becomes a creator. Bergson introduces the bold idea that the universe is not planned, but is evolving in unpredictable ways. God is not omnipotent, but limited by matter and by the will of its creations. This must be so, because evolution is only possible when there is freedom to choose. Freedom is a corollary of creation. By the same token God is not omniscient.

Man is godlike when he exercises his freedom, godlike whenever he creates. Every act of creation makes us free, different, and unique.

Bergson's works were put on the index of forbidden books by the Catholic Church in 1914, the same year in which he became a member of the French Academy.

EMERSON

Emerson's thinking about God and man was refreshingly unorthodox. He felt that Jesus was the most perfect teacher because he proved himself to be the most perfect man ever to walk the earth. He conceived of God as a moral force, the Soul that pervades the universe. Nature has its law, which is the law of things; but man has his own law, because he is a depository and representative on earth of this one, all-encompassing soul. Every man has a portion of the divine in him.

Like Kierkegaard, Emerson inveighs against the church that perpetuates ritual without imparting the divine spirit to its followers. A preacher's sermon should be the outcome of his own, deep religious experience. He should preach from within himself, not from without. Preaching frozen in dogma freezes the heart; it will not inspire the faithful; it not only fails to uplift thought, but actually profanes the divine.

True religion is continuous unfoldment. "Men have come to speak of revelation as something that occurred long ago, that is over and done with, as though God were dead." Revelation constantly flows to those capable of receiving it. Faith is enthusiasm, feeling for beauty, greatness and justice. Professions of faith should be singing of God in man.

Every man is an individual expression of the one, overall soul, which animates the universe. The more one wishes to partake of the soul, the more one will seek to develop the divine potential within him, the more he will strive to perfect himself, the more he will fulfill his task on earth. This was the essence of what Jesus taught.

"Alone in all history, he estimated the greatness in man. One man was true to what is in you and me. He saw that God incarnates Himself in man and evermore goes forth to take possession of His world."

Emerson's criticism that the clergy should not merely continue to carry on tradition, but should be animated by a sense of renewal, was extended to include man in general. His optimism about man's ability to grow spiritually was boundless. He felt that the layman, like the preacher, should free himself from the dead weight of history, from the idols of the past, and follow his own individual way, guided by intuition. He should seek new ways, tread new paths, be his own "wonderworker."

Self-reliance on liberation from the past is the second tenet of Emerson's teaching, the natural outcome of his attitude toward God, the church, and nature. Don't cling to any doctrine or sect, he says; don't try to imitate any great man. Be yourself! Imitators can only be second best, the shadow of someone else.

Listen to your own inspiration. "Dare to love God without a mediator."

Emerson's views on religion and life, his concept of God and man, obviously set him apart from adherents of traditional church practice and doctrine. In past centuries he would have been considered a heretic and treated as such. Fortunately, he was an American living in the nineteenth century. Though his views had great affinity with those of Bruno, who had been burned at the stake, Emerson escaped such a fate. Nevertheless, many were bewildered by his opinions; some were hostile to them. Realizing that his views were incompatible with those of his own church, he resigned his Unitarian pastorate in Boston's Old North Church.

Emerson's concept of God as a completely impersonal force, his insistence on faith rather than ritual, his reverence for any prophet who was inspired and able to inspire, whether he was called Moses, Zeus or Zoroaster, his belief that religions are good as long as man's spirit breathes in them, bring Emerson close to today's humanists. He was misunderstood and shunned by many, even some who were not men of the church. He accepted this fact equably. "Every man's words who speaks of that life (of wisdom) must sound vain to those who do not dwell in the same thought on their own part."

Yet there were many who were inspired by him. His teaching that it has been given to man to transcend himself, found enthusiastic followers. His religious eloquence was poetic, just as his poetry was religious. Both are pregnant with lofty visions, with deep philosophical content.

KIERKEGAARD

If ever a human being was obsessed and possessed by the concept of God as Judge, it was the Danish philosopher, Søoren Kierkegaard. His life was dominated by the doctrine of original sin and by the conviction that he must atone for it. It has been said that this strong sense of guilt was a legacy from his father, who had once cursed God for his hard life on the wasteland of Jutland.

The Lord thereupon took him to the city of Copenhagen, gave him wealth and a large family . . . only to strike him down at the height of his success. His wife and five of his children died young. Only one child, the future philosopher, survived.

He was a sickly child, with a birth defect, who was burdened with a conviction that he must expiate both his own sins and those of his father. He knew that he was doomed to die young, and accepted this fate willingly as a Christlike sacrifice to God. There is no doubt that this "redeemer complex" motivated all that he did. He believed that to be a Christian you must dedicate your whole life to Christ and endure hardship and suffering in his service.

There could be no compromise for him as regards the duty of a true Christian. As a member of the Lutheran Church, he was appalled to see its pastors living in great comfort. "Their sermons are good, and well constructed," he said, "but in eternity they are not read, but judged." Superficial religion, or mere ritual, would not do. All of Kierkegaard's writings are dedicated to the task of making Christians better understand the true essence of Christianity.

A Christian does not need to have God's existence proven to him. He has faith. Anything that must be proved is *ab ovo* to be regarded with suspicion. "To defend anything is to discredit it. He who defends it never believes it." The Christian religion is a religion of faith. The immaculate conception and the incarnation are the paradoxes of Christianity. We believe in the risen Christ because we wish to be immortal.

Religion is to Kierkegaard, as it was to Dostoevsky, a leap from the rational to the irrational. The *credo quia absurdum* of Saint Augustine is the creed of Kierkegaard, a theme that resounds like a motif of polyphonic music, the leitmotiv that accompanies him through life. Hence his lack of tolerance towards the established Church. There is nothing more difficult than to be a Christian in Christendom.

The Church must compromise between the tenets of religion and the practices of daily life, if it wants to survive. Kierkegaard would not admit that the average Christian is not blessed with the ability to see his destiny from the perspective of eternity, that most people's primary concern is to better their lives materially.

He who cannot compromise will perish. Kierkegaard knew this and was willing to accept the consequences of his uncompromising faith. He worked at his martyrdom; in fact, he worked himself to death. At forty, he was an old man, paralyzed in body and exhausted by the struggle to deserve ascension to his Christian Olympus, to be worthy of sitting down with Jesus Christ. As we said, his writings aimed at making people more conscious of what it means to be a true Christian.

Kierkegaard opposed Hegel because of the latter's postulate that thesis and antithesis unite in synthesis. To him, the opposite of Christianity was a denial of redemption. One is either a Christian or one is not. Man has to trust God completely. His model was Abraham, who was ready to sacrifice his son at God's command. This Biblical story brought Kierkegaard into opposition with Kant, who objected to such abject obedience. Kant thought that Abraham should have refused, because even God has no right to demand such an unnatural act.

Kierkegaard's Christian existentialism made an impact upon his own era which is still felt to this day. The Norwegian playwright, Ibsen, was greatly drawn to this heroic man. He used him as a model for the principal character of a play entitled "Brand." Brand, an ascetic priest and self-appointed prophet, is torn between duty and compassion, between the harsh demands of his faith and his human feelings. He refuses to go to his mother's deathbed unless she will surrender all her worldly goods, rather than the nine-tenths she proposes. His little boy, Eric, dies because he will not move to a warmer climate. He claims that his roots and his calling lie in that icy valley. In the end, Brand's wife goes too, unable to endure her husband's rigid demands. And Brand, like Kierkegaard, revolts against his own church, exhorting the people of the village to leave their church and climb the mountain, where they can worship God in a church without walls. He sways them at first, but ordinary people are unable to surmount the difficulties of exile, and cannot endure the hardships required of them. Tired, disappointed, they stone him and drive him up the mountain. He is an outcast, abandoned by all, and is finally alone with God.

Up on the icy peak, Brand finally realizes the error of his life. He had tried to reach perfection through the Will, by suppressing his human emotions. But man is not destined to be superhuman, and human perfection is unattainable. Caught in the path of an avalanche, Brand cries out, "Answer me, God, in the moment of death! If not by Will, how can man be redeemed?" and a voice is heard through the thunder: "He is a God of Love."

An American playwright, Edward Albee, has dealt with the same theme in his play, "Tiny Alice." His hero, like Kierkegaard, rejects his church as fallible and flawed. He seeks absolutes—the pure substance, the unadulterated Spirit. He is uncompromising and will not be satisfied with anything less than the Perfect Being which the word God can only feebly express. He dreams of martyrdom, of continuing the Redeemer's work on earth. His dream will be fulfilled: a mysterious force calls to him, his offering is accepted, and through the sacrifice of his pure life, the Church is purified.

Kierkegaard demonstrated by his own example that man cannot tolerate the Absolute. He had to die in moral solitude, like Brand, and like Julian, the hero of Albee's play. Here we see the flaw in all existentialist philosophy, religious as well as agnostic: preaching the supremacy of the will, it ignores the many forces and circumstances that determine human lives. Yet heroes of the Will are, indeed, the standard bearers of progress; like Moses, however, they die before they see the promised land.

Jean Paul Sartre's figure looms large in the twentieth century, just as Voltaire's did in the eighteenth and Victor Hugo's in the nineteenth. He is the prophet of a new faith—faith in man. Though it rejects ritual or any form of worship and holds out no promise of divine intervention, it is nevertheless religious in its fervor. Its basic tenet is that man must make himself. He was not given an essence at birth; he must define and develop one. This is man's task on earth, his burden and his responsibility. But self-determinism is also a very great privilege. God creates man as he creates all things; that is to say, man is not an object, the concept of which has preceded its existence.

"When we conceive of a creative God, we usually think of him as a superior artisan, and whatever doctrine we choose to consider, whether it is like that of Descartes or like that of Leibniz, it is always assumed that will follows reason, or at least accompanies it; that God always knows exactly what he intends to create. Thus, the concept of man, in the mind of God, can be likened to the concept of a paper knife in the mind of the manufacturer; God forms an idea and then produces man exactly as the manufacturer designs a paper-knife and produces it according to plan. Man is, therefore, but the materialization of an idea in the mind of God."[35]

If man were preconceived by God, what would become of human freedom? There would be a basic uniformity even though there might be different physical types; men of different races and colors, just as there are many varieties of dogs and birds which, within their own categories, are essentially the same. Animals pursue a certain way of life but they never surpass themselves; and useful objects serve a purpose which is predetermined in the mind of their maker.

Sartre rejects the notion that human nature follows a definite pattern. He believes it is unpredictable. Man eternally creates himself in complete freedom. The responsibility is his, and his alone: his goal should be to achieve nobility. Sartre excludes God, which makes his philosophy more coherent. "If God does not exist, there is at least one being for whom existence precedes essence, a being who exists before he can be defined in advance by any concept, and this being is man."

Man cannot turn to an omniscient and benevolent God to find out who he is. Each of us must establish his life-project without relying on God's assistance; in other words, we must act as though God did not exist. Sartre replaces God with humanistic ethics, qualifying his original postulate (that man must establish his own life-project) by saying that man's decisions must not disregard the well-being of others. Our actions must serve not only ourselves, but all mankind. Our private acts should be as virtuous as our public ones. Our criterion should be good faith. Then we can triumph over the inevitability of death; acting as our own stern judge, we shall fulfill our duty in the universe.

Though he excludes God from the process of man's becoming, Sartre's earnest insistence upon human ethics introduces religious overtones into his philosophy. He warns us that our actions testify unequivocally to the value of our lives, that they are judged by the whole universe. God loves man when man behaves as he would wish him to. God is in man when he fosters what is good. This is all that he requires of man.

In short, Sartre puts man on a pedestal, and gives him wings. Man—Icarus—must fly, though in nearing the sun he may singe his wings. His flight is symbolic; it is the soul which soars, in response to the call of a benevolent power. His rigorous logic, his demand for sincerity, and his faith in man make him a stern but basically optimistic philosopher, who believes the road to God is through man.

WHITEHEAD

Alfred North Whitehead had a truly universal mind. He was a belated offspring of the Renaissance, comparable in modern times only to Goethe. He was both a scholar of classical culture and a modern scientist, whose distinguised works include *Process and Reality*. In addition, he was coauthor with Bertrand Russell of *Principia Mathematica*. His diversified background prepared him for philosophy, the queen of arts, in which science and the humanities merge.

Whitehead's views on God and the universe are similar to those of Spinoza and Bergson. Like Bergson, he sees creation as continuous, and he shares Spinoza's conviction that God manifests himself through the universe. One of his Lowell lectures, "Science and Philosophy," was delivered at Harvard University in 1925. In it he said: "Neither physical nature nor life can be understood unless we fuse them together as essential factors in the composition of 'really real' things whose interconnections and individual characters constitute the universe."

A short time before his death in 1948, he discussed his ideas about God and the universe with his friend, Lucien Prince: "It was a mistake on the part of the Hebrews to imagine that God created the world from the outside, at one go. An all-foreseeing creator, who could have made the world as we find it now, what could we think of such a being? Foreseeing everything and yet putting into it all sorts of imperfections to redeem which it was necessary to send his only son into the world to suffer torture and hideous death; outrageous ideas . . ."

And further: "God is *in* the world or nowhere, creating continuously *in us and around us* [italics mine]. This creative principle is everywhere in animate and so-called inanimate matter, in the ether, water, earth, human hearts. But this creation is *a continuous process* [italics mine] and the process is the actuality, since no sooner do you arrive than you start on a fresh journey. Insofar as man partakes of this creative process does he partake of the divine, of God, and that participation is his immortality, reducing the question of whether his individuality survives death of the body to an irrelevancy. His true destiny as co-creator of the universe is his dignity and his grandeur."[36]

The above quotations summarize Whitehead's thought. God is *in* the universe. He does not say that God is also outside the universe. The universe is continuously created by the intelligence that pervades all. He uses the words "so-called inanimate matters" consciously, because he believes that even stone and metal are infused with divine intelligence; they too are both objects and actors in continuous creation. Everything is cause and effect at the same time. Whitehead rejects the story of Genesis as scientifically and logically unsound. In a subtle fashion, he also repudiates the notion that the soul survives after death. He shares Bergson's belief in creative evolution; the creative moment is immortal whatever the nature of creativity. Life is an eternal unfolding of creative moments, in each of which universal intelligence is asserting itself.

Man is what he does. Man partakes of the divine; that is, he rises above mere animality by using his share of the universal intelligence to create. Creating is the affirmation of life. Creating is affirming God. Man perpetuates himself in what he creates, for all creations have a concrete, as well as a symbolic value. The life of the universe is an epic of creation, a song with a refrain accompanied by infinite variations. The song of the individual is merging in the divine symphony. What is now will be gone the next moment, but it will remain an element of the universal creation; it is the yeast that will give rise to other creations. All present is eternity.

ADLER

Mortimer Adler calls himself a pagan, that is, one who does not believe in any of the so-called revealed religions. He adds, however, that he is "deeply concerned with the question of God's existence and with trying to establish the reasonableness of the belief in God." His book, *How to Think about God,* is an attempt to do just that.

Discussing the problem of the Prime Mover, of which Plato

and Aristotle speak, Adler asserts that there is no reason to assume the existence of a first cause because time has always existed in the infinity of the past and will always exist in the infinity of the future. Consequently, there was no beginning. "To say that there must have been some first cause—some uncaused cause in the series of causes and effects—is to assume that time is finite and that change, together with its causation, began with the operation of that first cause. This is the same as saying that the cosmos had a beginning. As we have seen, we must avoid that assumption because it begs the question. The opposite assumption, which is offered for our consideration, is not repugnant to reason. It is not repugnant to reason to assume that the cosmos has always existed, that there was no beginning to change or causation, that time is infinite, and that there is an infinite series of causes and effects. In such a series, there is no first cause" (p. 41).

So far as reason can tell, the nonexistence of God would leave the phenomena of nature unaffected. Both what happened and the explanation of what happened would remain the same. Yet, to renounce all speculation about natural phenomena, to say that experimental observation of causes and effects explains everything, is to abdicate the right of reason to inquiry. It would be remiss in its duty, which is never to be satisfied while any mystery remains. If one can neither establish any proof of God's existence by refined thinking, nor can one be satisfied with renouncing all inquiry about it, what is the philosopher to do?

Adler advances what he calls the cosmological argument. Since the cosmos has always existed, one must infer that there is a force that sustains and upholds it. The principle of inertia—which assumes that bodies remain motionless unless some outside force sets them in motion, or that bodies in motion continue to move unless some outside force makes them cease to move—does not apply to the cosmos because it has not been created (it has always existed).

Here some digression is necessary. Adler explains that all

112

parts of the cosmos are perishable, but their disappearance represents only a transmutation, a change of state; the cosmos as a whole is not affected by the transmutation of its parts. Adler calls things in the cosmos superficially contingent because their contingency represents but a change, not the substance of the cosmos. If, on the other hand, the whole of the cosmos were to disappear, its parts would perish with it—the whole would sink into nothingness. The cosmos is, as Adler puts it, radically contingent.

But the cosmos exists—beyond reasonable doubt. Therefore, there must, be some supernatural force which sustains and upholds it.

This reasoning leads us to the conclusion that God is not the creator, but the sustainer of the universe. His force is not a creative, but a preservative force.

The cosmological argument allows Adler to bridge the gap between philosophical and sacred theology. Philosophy can derive conclusions from this argument that are similar to those advanced by traditional belief. One such conclusion is that the upholder of the universe must be omnipotent because if it were not, that would allow for a greater force, which then would be God. The supernatural force that prevents the cosmos from sinking into nothingness is supreme. Being supreme is tantamount to being omnipotent.

This supreme being must be thought of as an intelligent being who knows and wills what it is doing. Adler advises us not to interpret such a being in an anthropomorphic sense, as many religious people do. Using such words as "knowing" and "willing," Adler avers that God knows and wills in a way that is different from human beings.

Arriving at this point, the philosopher asks: Where do we go from here? What is man's relation to the Supreme Being? Adler's answer: Man's essence is analogous to the Divine in the sense that man is more intelligent than any other animal on earth. In this sense man is made in God's image. Man, like God, is a person, not a thing, meaning that man can think and

113

embrace the cosmos in his thoughts. The other living beings on earth are, in this sense, considered as things.

Philosophical reasoning has brought us closer to traditional religious thought, dogmas apart. We have arrived at "the edge of the chasm." We ourselves must decide whether we wish to remain there, in the domain of philosophy, or make the leap, as Pascal did, to the other side of the bridge, into the realm of faith.

The Balance Sheet of Philosophy

Speculative philosophy, considered separately from social or political philosophy, concerns itself with the universe, and with man and his position in the universe. Religion deals with these same problems, but, whereas religion comes up with final answers which are unproven yet not to be disputed, philosophy appeals to the inquiring mind, because it demands rational arguments. The difficulty for philosophers is that the very sort of questions they ask will elude irrefutable proof. The approach to them varies with each philosopher; even when their answers are the same, the connotation of their conclusions may be different.

Plato's and Aristotle's Prime Mover, the First Cause which is no effect at the same time, is not the same as Spinoza's; Christianity is not the same to Hegel as it is to Pascal, and it is different still to Kierkegaard.

Moreover, the statements of the philosophers concerning God and the universe are influenced by the epoch in which they lived, and by the governments which they lived under. Descartes would probably have expostulated more freely about the Creator and his creation had he lived in the Age of Enlightenment; Voltaire, on the other hand, would have been forced to restrain himself—he would not have dared to express his contempt for the Church had he lived a century earlier, in Descartes' time. Spinoza's teaching—that God can change nothing, being subject to his own law, and that he is neither omniscient nor the initiator of things transient, would have been anathema during the time of the Inquisition. Nevertheless, history shows that philosophers have generally been sincere and courageous in manifesting their views. Bruno was willing to burn at the stake rather than recant—as was Servetus, and many others followed their example.

Philosophy Versus Religion

We have stated the basic difference between religion and philosophy, namely that the first claims to be revealed, the second to be the result of man's reasoning. This explains the different attitude that philosophers have toward their audience. Religion teaches the revealed truth, and maintains that it is not to be questioned. Philosophy tries to demonstrate, to convince. Plato, Aristotle, and others, concluded that the law of causality must stop somewhere, that there was a first cause, from which all others are derived. This was the end of their speculation in that direction. They did not seek to elaborate the relations of that First Cause to man, nor to find out its nature or its attributes.

Pascal, on the other hand, having accepted the doctrine of God, the Father, who sent his only son to redeem mankind, renounced scientific thinking, listening instead to reasons of the heart, as he put it. Albert Camus, a disciple of Dostoevsky, shares with the Russian writer a concern for justice, both divine and human; but he parts company with Dostoevsky when the latter chooses to throw himself on the mercy of God and "leaps into the irrational," as Camus puts it, rather than rebel against injustice, cosmic or human.

Philosophy, like science, knows that its conclusions are subject to error. The philosopher suffers anguish, for, despite his dedication to the search for truth, he realizes that the ultimate answers will always elude him. The philosopher never speaks "ex cathedra," knowing, as he does, that his statements are neither infallible or divinely inspired. Philosophy never condemns heresy, but rather, welcomes it.

115

Religion is never wrong, whereas no philosophy claims to be perfect. Philosophy has no need to erect churches—when it does, as in the case of Auguste Comte, it becomes a religion. The French Revolution of 1789 eliminated religion, but established the cult of the Supreme Being, and, by so doing, established a new religion. Philosophy has no dogma, but serves as a guide in our life and thinking, replacing divine assistance. Philosophy is a science, for it uses scientific methods to arrive at its conclusions. Philosophy is the science of thinking. It is the queen of sciences because it gathers various branches of science together to form a whole, in which each has its proper place.

Philosophy says nothing about life beyond the grave because it knows nothing and can prove nothing about it.

Philosophy contemplates the infinite with awe. Philosophy is religious when it restricts its thinking to the basic and eternal questions about God, the universe, and man. Like religion, it transcends the ephemeral and embraces timelessness, only to return to the mortal sphere; thus it fluctuates between the infinite and the finite, from the universe to man.

Philosophy is truly catholic, being universal. Philosophy extols man's ability to relate to the universe and to relate from the universe to himself. No man can lead a commendable life without a minimum amount of philosophy, without giving thought to what he is and why he is here. Man, says Goethe, must constantly renew himself, constantly die and be reborn through meditation; otherwise, he will be only a troublesome visitor on this murky planet. Pascal remarks: "Man is but a frail reed, but he is a thinking reed."

The Influence of Philosophy

The aim of philosophy is to be a guide to man's behavior as an individual and as a member of society. It should make life more harmonious and contribute to the formation of a better, more just and perfect society.

Philosophy must deal with the same problems as religion,

that is, the existence of a Creator and man's relation to Him, but its approach is different. Philosophy is more closely related to science, inasmuch as it attempts to interpret scientific discoveries, using these facts and phenomena as the basis for a more comprehensible view of life and the universe. One can state that science influences philosophy, and philosophy influences religion. Indeed, any advanced religion is necessarily imbued with philosophy.

Philosophical ideas are as good as the actions based upon them. Plato conceived of a smoothly functioning society, ruled by the best element. This idea germinated throughout the ages, bringing about diverse attempts to create a better society, such as monarchy "by the grace of God," meaning absolute rule by a single individual, then constitutional monarchy, and eventually a democratic republic. The same idea gave rise, for example, to Proudhonism, which tried to eliminate the profit system and replace it with a sort of barter economy. It culminated in Communism, conceived by the philosophers Marx and Engels, which has brought about profound changes in the social setup of many nations. Philosophy degenerated into Nietzcheism, the product of a demented philosopher who insisted on the right of the strongest to rule. Nietzcheism was eagerly adopted by the German national-socialists, who justified their determination to rule the world by claiming to be the master race. The Superman theory was discussed by the Russian writer, Feodor Dostoevsky, who early recognized it as the theory that would do away with ethical considerations of any kind. The many millions who suffered and perished in World War II are testimony to the fact that ideas born in the mind of a single individual can profoundly affect the lives of many.

Philosophers sometimes give voice to ideas that have been present in the minds of many but have not been expressed. Thus the *Philosophical Dictionary* of Voltaire and his fellow philosophers of the 18th century gave articulation to popular feeling and helped to pave the way for the great French Revolution in 1789. Montesquieu, French historian, philosopher, and author of "The Spirit of the Laws," deeply influenced those who drafted the American Constitution. Rousseau's concept of the "noble savage," as expounded in his novel, *Emile,* created a new movement in French education, a movement hostile to the traditional methods, which were based on forming the minds of the young. An even greater contribution was the prize-winning essay which he submitted to the Academy of Dijon, denouncing the dehumanizing effect of technological progress. He was the first to point out this danger, which has now become even more serious.

In matters of human behavior and ethics, philosophy was a supreme teacher. The Stoics taught us that man should face with dignity whatever befalls him in life. Equanimity was the motto of Epictetus, the slave. It was this word that Antonius the Emperor is said to have bequeathed to his successor, Marcus Aurelius. The teaching of the Stoics enabled virtuous people to live and endure the oppression of tyrannical emperors.

Plato's ideal, that the noblest should rule, was realized during the administrations of the Antonines and of Seneca. These three philosophers were given the power to try out their ideas, and they stood the test brilliantly. All three of them proved that Utopia is not necessarily an impossible dream—that what is needed is virtue at the helm of state. Philosophy in action can work, but sincere and effective administrators are the ingredient without which no attempt to better mankind can succeed.

Chapter V

OF GOOD AND EVIL

DEFINITION OF GOOD

Generally speaking, one can define good as something that benefits mankind. In a narrower sense, we call that good which benefits people without hurting anyone. And good has several aspects. There is personal good when I help an individual; there is social good when I support a cause which I believe will be beneficial to people or to a community. There is social good also in compassionate aid to those less fortunate than we are, and in causes which serve to enlighten the human mind. The greatest good is that which is done out of love, out of human solidarity, that which aims at human freedom and justice.

THE RELATIVITY OF GOOD

In practical experience, the concept of good among people and nations differs greatly. Speaking of right and wrong, Pascal declared that what was right on this side of the Pyrenees might be wrong on the other side. He meant that people judge good and evil not on general principles but on the basis of their own particular experience, their own beliefs, or their own personal interests.

This fact is abundantly demonstrated by history. Aggressive nations justify their territorial ambitions by invoking their need for national security, and the people usually support their governments in this view. Wars are always fought for a just cause, even when the desire for conquest may be the sole reason for waging them. When people were tortured and burned at the stake during the Holy Inquisition, it was claimed that such barbarous actions were committed to save men's souls. The most villainous actions might be dressed in the garb of justice. Hitler's extermination of six million Jews was supposed to preserve racial purity, and the deportation of entire populations by Stalin was carried out to defend the revolution against traitors.

Since good and evil are man-made concepts, human actions may be judged good by some and evil by others. Workers laid off because they are no longer necessary in this era of robots are an illustration. Chance happenings may be fortunate in the view of some, unfortunate in the view of others. The death of an individual is a blow to his family, but could be a stroke of luck for the person who takes over his job. Adversity bears the adjective "bad," luck is called "good" fortune. No moral value is attached to such events.

In order to classify an event as good or evil, we must consider its effect upon the person involved. One individual, if he inherited a fortune, might be morally and physically corrupted by sudden wealth. On the other hand, what seems to be a disastrous event may turn out to be a blessing in disguise. Feodor Dostoevsky, was condemned to death for his revolutionary activities. At the last minute, the death sentence was commuted to long-term imprisonment. Out of this personal tragedy came a deep religiosity which was the inspiration for his greatest works.

In these days, many active in politics or in private business go through a moral crisis and turn to the hope and solace of religion. Theological schools in the United States have reported an increasing enrollment of middle-aged or older students during the last several years of the 1970s.

GOOD AS A LESSER EVIL

An even more dramatic example of the relativity of good and evil is the case of Harry S. Truman, who was President of the

United States toward the end of World War II. American and foreign scientists working together had just perfected the atomic bomb. The war was still raging and could go on a lot longer, costing hundreds of thousands of young lives. Using the bomb would probably end it quickly. But the unleashing of this awesome weapon would destroy tens of thousands instantly, and set a dangerous precedent in human warfare. Still, there was almost a certainty that the shock and terror of the bomb would force Japan to surrender, thus saving many American lives. The President was faced with an appalling situation. Either alternative was certain to entail enormous suffering. And so, this good and honorable man sanctioned the horrible destruction of some hundred thousand civilians, and the maiming of others who must live on with atrocious wounds or a lingering cancer.

Obviously, in a situation like this, one must try to choose the lesser of two evils.

THE AMBIVALENCE OF HUMAN NATURE

The cult of the Egyptian god Iris or Serapis, as he was called in Rome, symbolized life that ends and is renewed eternally. It could also symbolize human nature, which oscillates between constructive and destructive impulses. The human mind is curious and often wayward. Following one path, we humans want to know where the opposite path leads.

The philosopher Kant speaks of a categorical imperative —man's innate need to obey the absolute law of his conscience regardless of circumstances. Rousseau believed that man is born good and that civilization corrupts him, creating a desire for power and wealth and arousing jealousy, selfishness, and other evils.

Actually the opposite is true. Man is born selfish, as all creatures are, because the instinct of self-preservation urges him to combat forces that threaten his survival. However, civili-

121

zation, which compels him to live with others, teaches him that it is to his own advantage to consider other people's interests so that others will be willing to help him in the struggle for survival. Dostoevsky, who knew human nature as did few others, endowed many of his characters with ambivalent emotions. In his novel, *The Eternal Husband,* a man meets another who had been his wife's lover. That other man visits him in his house. During the night, the guest has an attack of the liver; his host nurses him devotedly. But when he thinks that the sick man is asleep, he tries to murder him. In another of his novels, *The Idiot,* the relationship between Prince Myshkin and Rogozhin is similar to that of the Eternal Husband and his rival. Rogozhin is jealous of the Prince because the woman whom he loves insanely regards him as inferior to the Prince. Rogozhin represents brutal, carnal passion, while the Prince typifies saintly and compassionate love. Rogozhin follows the Prince like a shadow, invites him to his house, exchanging crosses with him as a sign of brotherhood, even takes him to his mother for her blessing. Later, he lurks in a corner near the Prince, waiting to stab him.

The average human being is a mixture of good and evil propensities; outside influences, such as education and experience, or hereditary traits, cause him to lean in one or the other direction. There are, however, persons in whom goodness or wickedness so predominate that the opposite instinct is almost completely absent. History, both ancient and recent, supplies us with examples of both.

VIRTUE IN ACTION

Confucius
The Chinese philosopher Confucius was born in the middle of the sixth century B.C. His family was of lofty descent, but had come down in the world. His father, who was commandant of the Tsow district in the state of Lu (part of the modern

Shantung), died when the boy was only three years old. His widow, though left in poor circumstances, saw to it that the boy received good training, especially in the rigorous Chinese customs and ceremonials. The boy's love of learning enabled him to make the most of a good education. For years his poverty compelled him to labor at menial tasks. Then he began his career as a teacher, not settling anywhere, but traveling about and instructing a small number of disciples who had gathered around him. His fame as a man of learning spread over the entire principality of Lu. The death of his mother, which occurred in 527 B.C., strengthened people's respect for him because of the depth and sincerity with which he performed his filial duty as a mourner. His observance thereof established a custom which was maintained for twenty-five centuries, until the Communists' advent to power. They repudiated Confucius and what he stood for, though they could not completely eradicate his influence from Chinese life.

Confucius lived near the end of the Chow dynasty when, after many centuries, feudalism had become deeply rooted in China. In that day, every form of intrigue and vice was rampant. It seemed to Confucius that the only remedy for this widespread immorality was to be found in trying to revive the principles and precepts of the holy sages of antiquity. He therefore lectured to his pupils on the ancient works, historical and constitutional, with which he himself was familiar. And in addition, *he taught the great power of example,* enjoining each individual to observe carefully his duties toward parents and state. A ruler, he said, can only be great if he himself lives an exemplary life. The morality of the leader will be imitated by his followers.

At age 52, Confucius was appointed magistrate, and the year after, minister of crime in Lu province. Wonderful success crowned his administration. Reforms were introduced, justice was fairly dispensed, and crime almost wiped out in the state. Unfortunately, intrigues of those who had been dislodged from positions of power by his administration forced Confucius to

123

leave office. The reign of virtue which he had inaugurated ceased with his departure, but the people continued to admire him. He died in the state which he had tried to transform into a model society. He was buried in a magnificent tomb which became a place of pilgrimages for centuries.

Confucius left us nothing in writing. His sayings have come down to us through his disciples. What is important to us is the fact that one man alone, without help from anyone, could transform the institutions of his state by his teaching and by the example of his own life. His basic tenet, that all people in all places have to fulfill their responsibilities in a spirit of kindness and piety, was easy for people to understand. Confucianism became a state-upholding doctrine, a concrete example of what we call *good*.

Confucius is said to be the author of the Golden Rule: "Act toward others as you would others act towards you," a solid, viable principle and guide in human relations. This principle was exalted by the twentieth century philosopher, Martin Buber, in his "I am Thou" concept.

Seneca

In the first century of our era, the Roman philosopher Seneca became first the tutor, and then the all-powerful minister of the young emperor Nero. Seneca had learned wisdom from Greek and Latin masters—Pythagorean and Stoic—who taught him chastity, moderation in eating and drinking, the pursuit of a purposeful life.

When Seneca became the teacher and preceptor of the most important personage in the empire, he directed his efforts toward making his pupil a morally and intellectually healthy man, capable of living up to the all-important role for which he was destined. The task was not easy; he had to combat both the hereditary tendencies of his pupil and the intrigues of his mother, Agrippina (who was determined to keep her son dependent on her). Against great odds, Seneca managed to gain more and more influence over his young pupil. He showed him the glory of being admired as a virtuous and wise man, and possibly a great ruler.

For Nero's inauguration, Seneca composed a speech, which the new emperor was to read in the Roman Senate. It was remarkable for its content as well as its spirit, and revealed clearly its author's political views. In that speech, Nero declared that he was to hold power with the approval of the Senate and the unanimous vote of the army. He said that to govern well, he would need good advice and good examples. His government would in many respects differ from the previous one (that of Claudius): he would permit no arbitrary justice, would abolish bribery, would not try to settle all trials himself, would not choke off debates nor indulge in favoritism. The Senate would be called upon to exercise its traditional functions as a legislative body. Italy and Rome would be under the jurisdiction of the consuls and the Senate. The emperor would reserve only one post for himself, that of commander-in-chief of the army.

The speech was a wise one, inspired by Seneca's idealism. Essentially, it laid down, nineteen hundred years ago, the principles upon which a modern democracy is founded. The speech was received by the Senate with a tumultuous ovation. It voted that the entire speech be engraved on a silver column, and that it should be read every year when new consuls came into office.

When Seneca became Nero's chief minister, our philosopher-statesman went to work to translate his views on government into reality. He made a clean sweep of the old judicial system and did away with the practice of denunciations. He protected his magistrates from arbitrary intervention. Juries deliberated freely; Seneca's motto was "The law above all," which could be translated in modern times as "No one above the law." An accused person was considered innocent until proven guilty. That was 1200 years before the British Magna Carta.

His pupil, the monarch, enthusiastically embraced the principles taught by his revered teacher. The legend says that, as he was about to sign his first death warrant, he declared that he was sorry he had ever learned to sign his name.

Seneca's solicitude extended even to the slaves. He had a law passed whereby slaves were henceforth to be allowed to lodge complaints against their masters if they had suffered excessive severity or cruelty. Moreover, the owners were accountable for the lives of their slaves. Thus, the wisdom of the sage inspired the action of the legislator. During the five years that Seneca was in power, the Roman empire enjoyed a millenium. Historians speak of it as the "Quinquennium Neronis," the period of happiness and perfection of young Nero. It would be more appropriate to call it "quinquennium Senecae," for it was he who transformed a chaotic administration into an orderly and beneficial one.

Gandhi

Gandhi, called the Mahatma (the Great Souled), the sage and saint of India, frail in body but indomitable in spirit, fought the British Empire and led his people to independence without ever resorting to violence. In his battle of right against might, he marched twenty-four days—two hundred and forty-one miles—to break a lump of salt from the sea, and thus break the Salt Law imposed by the British. This law came to symbolize, for him and for India, the unjust use of naked power. Gandhi marched at the head of the procession; hundreds of millions of Indians watched this man who believed that the power of the word is stronger than the power of the gun. Leaves were strewn across his path, and wherever he went, the smallest town filled up with onlookers who watched breathtakingly the awesome struggle waged by him, hoping for his triumph. And when the great march was accomplished, the continent of India awakened: everywhere the spirit of disobedience to colonial rule was manifested, foreign cloth was burned, the women started to spin on the wheel, the spirit of independence was buoyed, a flame that people did not know was glimmering in them—the flame of human pride, of dignity—flared up after this manifestation and proclamation of the need for Good in the human world. With this Salt March that took place from

March 11 to April 5, 1930, the British grip on India was practically broken. One man's will, faith in justice, a saintly belief in Good accomplished this.

All three of the men we have described had deep personal convictions, and each had far-reaching effects on the world of their day. Confucius left an imprint on Chinese society which lasted for centuries. Seneca, like Confucius, transformed a corrupt society into a moral and harmonious one. Gandhi was motivated by the same sense of brotherhood as Seneca. He spoke for the untouchables, while Seneca spoke for the slaves; both pleaded for compassion toward "our unfortunate brothers."

These men did their utmost, but the principles they had established became corrupted and were eventually abandoned. Human beings need the example and discipline of dedicated leaders in order to continue in doing good. In the eternal struggle between the principles of good and evil, we must salute even a temporary victory of the good as a beacon of hope for mankind, a proof that the destructive forces which threaten our survival can be overcome. To be good is infinitely more important than to be knowledgeable, for—as Pascal says—"Physical science will not console me for the ignorance of morality in time of affliction, but the science of ethics will always console me for ignorance of physical science."

Saint Kolbe

The most admirable, most heroic affirmation of good in the face of evil was made by a Catholic priest named Kolbe, who was at Auschwitz. A prisoner had escaped from Block 14. As punishment, other members of that block were forced to stand at attention all day without even their usual inadequate rations. Finally, a soup cauldron was brought, but the contents were sadistically poured onto the ground. The second day, ten victims were selected for reprisal; they would die in the starvation bunker. Among them was a man named Gajowniczek.

127

When his turn came, he cried out, "My poor wife, poor children, goodbye."

No. 16670 stepped forward and approached the camp's deputy commander.

"I would like to die in the place of one of these men," Kolbe said.

"And in whose place would you like to die?"

"The one with the wife and chidren."

"And who are you?" the commander asked.

"A Catholic priest."

His request was granted. The Roman Catholic Church heard the story, which was later confirmed by survivors who had witnessed the scene. Kolbe was canonized on October 10, 1982. The priest's noble act nullified the attempt of the Nazis to reduce men to the level of animals. It demonstrated the superiority of good over evil, for it is easy to commit evil deeds, but extremely difficult to find the courage to do what Father Kolbe did.

EVIL IN ACTION

Hitler and Stalin

These two can be discussed together, although they represent opposite poles of social and political persuasion. The fact is, they had many characteristics in common. Both hated democracy, because of their contempt for the masses. Both were madmen, but nevertheless shrewd politicians. Both were insanely suspicious and did away with their early supporters; both lived in isolation from the people and were difficult to approach. Both were vulgar, uneducated men who hated intellectuals. Both were authoritarian, and both lived in a dream world, refusing to face reality.

Stalin and Hitler made a deal for the dismemberment of Poland, dividing the spoils between them. That started World War II. War was the inevitable outcome of Hitler's accession to power, for war was his element. He had been a failure in life, and war gave him the opportunity to avenge himself. War is the world of killing, a world in which morality has no place. Hitler was completely amoral; he loathed the rules that regulated the lives of civilized people. He resented the fact that Judeo-Christian morality had been imposed on the German people far back in the ninth century by Charlemagne. He took out his anger and resentment on the Jews because the Jews were defenseless. Through them he aimed at Christianity; in fact, he incarcerated many Christian priests.

The record is damning! Hitler's attack on Poland was the beginning of World War II. It cost some seven million German lives, twenty-eight million Russian lives, exacted countless other sacrifices across the world. It left Germany in ruins and the continent of Europe exhausted. Six million Jews from various countries of Europe that were occupied by Hitler's armies died in the gas chambers erected by German scientists.

The reign of Adolf Hitler lasted for twelve years, but this relatively short time was sufficient to transform the continent of Europe into a living hell. Never before in history had any tyrant heaped so much indignity on his victims, not even the Mongols or other conquerors who enslaved those whom they defeated. Nazi officials vied with each other in inventing more and more refined types of cruelty. Their intent was to subject their victims to the greatest possible suffering, and particularly to deprive them of all human dignity and hope. Never has the human mind visualized such hell as that conjured up by Hitler and his henchmen.

Germany, once called "the land of poets and thinkers," had come to that. Evil as a destructive human characteristic was amply demonstrated during the twelve years of Hitler's reign. Subsequent generations, viewing the films which depict his regime, will surely profit by this horrible example. It will show them the abyss awaiting them if they listen to preachers of extreme nationalism and to demagogic propaganda of hatred.

Stalin is the obvious counterpart of the German devil. Like

Hitler, he sent millions of people to death camps, established a police state at home, and deported entire populations.

Solzhenitsyn, in his book *The Gulag Archipelago,* describes Stalin's crimes more eloquently than anyone else. In the chapter "The Slave Caravans," he mentions "red trains"; prisoners were sent to camps in red cattle cars. He writes:

> The red trains were always a help when the courts in some particular place were working swiftly or the transit facilities were overcrowded. It was possible in this way to dispatch a large number of prisoners in one batch. That is how millions of peasants were transported in 1929–1931. That is how they exiled Leningrad from Leningrad. That is how they populated the Kolyma in the thirties: every day Moscow, the capital of our country, belched out one such train to Sovetskaya Gavan, to Vanino Port. And each provincial capital also sent off red trainloads, but not on a daily schedule. That is how they removed the Volga German Republic to Kazakhstan in 1941, and later, all the rest of the exiled nations were sent off the same way. In 1945 Russia's prodigal sons and daughters were sent from Germany, from Czechoslovakia, from Austria, and simply from western border areas—whoever had gotten there on his own—in such trains as these.

In the preceding chapter, entitled "The Ports of Archipelago," Solzhenitsyn reveals what happened to the prisoners in the camp:

> General assignment work, that is the main and basic work performed in any given camp. Eighty percent of the prisoners work at it, and they all die off. All. And they bring new ones in, to take their places, and they again are sent to general assignment work. Doing this work, you expend the last of your strength. And you are always hungry. And always wet. And shoeless. And you are given short rations and short everything else. And put in the worst barracks. And they won't give you any treatment when you're ill. The only ones who survive in the camps are those who succeed, by bribery or by any other means, in avoiding being put on general assignment work.[1]

In the above lines the entire Stalin regime is laid bare, with its extreme cruelty and utter disregard for human life. The prison camps of the Gulag Archipelago are mirror images of Dachau, Auschwitz, Treblinka and other Nazi camps. Hitler and Stalin were brothers in evil. These two fiends had a natural sympathy for each other. Stalin made a pact with Hitler to divide Poland between them; he trusted very few, but he trusted Hitler—to the extent that he disregarded the warnings of his own secret service, that Hitler was preparing to attack him. He dismissed these reports as British propaganda.

Ill-gotten gains never bring lasting satisfaction. Hitler, who set the world afire, ended his own life with a bullet. Stalin lived in constant fear and, after his death, Krushchev, who called him a bloodthirsty tyrant, had his body removed from his mausoleum.

Dr. Mengele

Both good and evil individuals find imitators. This fact increases the responsibility of each of us for our actions. Some are corrupted by power. A case in point is Dr. Mengele, called "The Black Angel" by inmates of Auschwitz. It was he who decided whether new arrivals would be sent to the gas chambers or be allowed to die more slowly from exhaustion, starvation or illness. His down-turned thumb meant immediate death, as it did at the Roman circus, where spectators had used this sign to indicate that fate of defeated gladiators. Survivors of the camp described Mengele as a strikingly handsome man and an able physician with soft and skillful hands. This man obviously had in him a great potential for good, which unfortunately was subverted by an even greater potential for evil. Had he lived in a country where there was justice and respect for human life, Dr. Mengele might have become a benefactor to society and to mankind. The regime under which he lived gave him the power to destroy human lives with impunity.

Thus he succumbed to the satanic side of his nature, using his ability to do good only to refine his wickedness to a high degree of perversion. He enjoyed showing himself as benevolent, raising hope and gratitude in the hearts of people, then crushing them with a single blow. He would deliver pregnant women with great skill and solicitude, and when he held the baby in his arms, he would throw it to the floor and step on it. He attended to sick people in the hospital, and when they felt better, sent them to the gas chambers. He derived voluptuous enjoyment from the shock and horror of the victims of his sophisticated crimes.

In the files of Mengele one finds accusations that he shocked the inmates of the concentration camp with electricity, to see how much current they could stand; that he exposed a group of nuns to extreme X-ray radiation, injected deadly fluid into eyes, that he castrated or sterilized hundreds of inmates, that he shot female prisoners and cut off parts of their bodies to be used as culture material for experiments. Even more horrible deeds are told about him which one hesitates to repeat because they pass the limit of human revulsion.

Mengele personified the concept of Evil; he fitted the portrait of the Anti-Christ as depicted in medieval chronicles. He can be considered as the most evil figure, surpassing even Hitler and Stalin in his total disregard for the value of human life. The crimes of those dictators were motivated by fear, jealousy or political considerations, while Mengele killed and maimed his victims for the sheer pleasure of doing evil—disguised as medical curiosity. Yet, thanks to the protection of highly placed individuals in various countries, he had managed to elude capture and died in freedom.

INDIFFERENCE IS THE ACCOMPLICE OF EVIL

Someone has said that the opposite of good is not evil, but indifference. That is to say, evildoers succeed whenever there is widespread public apathy. A woman was attacked on the street in New York, and her screams were ignored by passers-by because they "did not want to get involved."

Indifference is one of the fundamental causes of all evil. War is the most inhuman of all crimes, yet wars have been unceasing in human history. There has hardly been a time when one could speak of "pax in terris"—a global peace. Somewhere on the planet man has always been pitted against man. Killing in war is considered a virtue. The twentieth century has seen warfare on a global scale, each war more destructive than the last.

As the century nears its end, mankind is threatened by nuclear war on land, sea, underwater, and even in outer space—and all this because we have yet to learn that mankind is one, that what we do to others is bound to backfire against US.

Religions teach that one should love one's neighbor as oneself. This is contrary to human nature, but it is not only possible, it is imperative to care for one's neighbor. Technical progress has brought nations closer but has not brought more harmonious human relations. We had our fill of horrors in two world wars; they were fought because we did not prevent them. Great wars may come to an end, but small wars, feuds, terrorism, and torture have become routine. Indifference, sister of hypocrisy, fosters these evils.

We, as Americans, have our own doctrines, our ideology and moral principles. We combat those who oppose them, but in fighting one evil we let another evil—the opposite extreme—prevail. We went to war to defeat German National Socialism, which preached the superiority of the German race, reduced German women to the level of brood hens, regarded humans as expendable, and aimed at the subjugation of "inferior" peoples. Yet we, the professed champions of human dignity, of human value and personal freedom, did not prevent the degradation and extermination of six million Jews, and of other prisoners in Nazi camps. Worse still, no nation was willing to offer refuge to those who had escaped the Nazis in a leaky ship and were going from port to port seeking refuge. They sank with their ship—men, women, and children—while the champions of human freedom believed that they were righteous and good, and fighting a just war.

133

It has been established that the Allies knew about the gas chambers in Nazi concentration camps, yet they did nothing to save the unfortunate victims. The champions of human freedom were indifferent to the fate of the millions who suffered torments unprecedented in human history.

When the war was over, the new enemy of human liberty was Communism. The United States, citadel of freedom, helped overthrow Communist or radical regimes in Guatemala and Chile, but averted its eyes when it came to the regimes of terror that succeeded them. Death squads, assassinations, terrorism, and oppressive governments were tolerated because they were anticommunist; but they, too, were evil and often worse than the governments they supplanted.

Loyalty to principles must be demonstrated, not merely professed. We shall be judged by our deeds!

Indifference is abdication of responsibility. Evil will continue as long as we remain indifferent to wrongs done to others.

Responsibility rests not only with government; in the last analysis, we as individuals are responsible for crime and injustice everywhere in the world.

Man's primary task is to create a world in which human creativity will promote peace and the welfare of all. We are conscience stricken when we give bread to our children, knowing that in Africa, Asia, and elsewhere children die of starvation every day. In the spring of 1984 there were food riots in the Dominican Republic. The following is an excerpt from the *Los Angeles Times:*

> There is no welfare, no unemployment insurance, and for most, no work. Some of the children here are said to live and die without ever tasting a drop of milk. The impoverished, said one Dominican, face daily life with three choices: they live off their friends, they live off their family, or they die.

The same situation prevails in many countries of Africa and Asia. Even in the opulent United States there are at the time of this writing several millions who are hungry and have no place to go. One must ask: What kind of civilization is ours which is built on the misery of the majority of mankind? We cannot escape the answer that it is a false and cruel civilization. No wonder nations choose to eliminate at least hunger, even though it means the loss of their freedom.

THE RESPONSIBILITY OF THE INTELLECTUALS

In 1927 a book was published in France under the title *La Trahison des Clerks (The Treason of the Intellectuals)*. In it, the author, Julien Benda, defended French intellectual tradition against modern literary trends. The title of the book could well apply to the behavior of certain French intellectuals during World War II. A number of writers rallied to the fascist regime of Marshall Philippe Pétain, installed by the Germans. In Germany, most of the intellectuals betrayed the ideals of Western civilization and took up the slogans of German fascism. Attempting to justify his treason, the dramatist Gerhart Hauptmann declared: "One cannot protect oneself against a downpour with an umbrella," meaning that an individual writer was helpless against the powerful and popular advocates of National Socialism.

Yet Thomas Mann, the most respected of German writers, exiled himself rather than follow Hauptmann's example. He spoke to his compatriots by radio from abroad, warning them that the course they had taken would be disastrous for Germany. In Germany an underground was formed to fight Hitler, but it was too late. France, on the other hand, established its underground early, and actively cooperated with the Free French Forces and Allied England.

Individuals, like nations, show what they are worth in times of trial. The Scandinavian nations—Denmark, Norway, and Sweden—repudiated Nazism in the most categorical manner, defying the formidable power of Hitler's forces, then at their peak. Denmark, occupied by the Nazis, refused to cooperate with them. The Danish king was ostentatious in his resistance, giving his people an example of moral courage. In Norway there was one individual, by the name of Quisling, who served as a puppet of the Nazis; his name became a generic word for "traitor," written with a small "q" and passed into every modern language. Once the war was over, Sweden showed itself humane and generous with the victims of the Nazis by offering shelter and long-term help to the survivors of the concentration camps.

In the title of the book referred to above, the word "clerk," in its archaic meaning, designated a man of letters or an educated person, and also implied a person who had some official function. In fact, educated and intelligent people ought to feel a sense of obligation; they are the grown-ups in society and have a duty to insist upon justice, compassion, and human solidarity. They must advance humane laws and social institutions. The masses are the children of society, and the "clerks" must care for them because they have been endowed with more intelligence and have had the advantage of a good education. Unfortunately, the vast majority of the intelligentsia thinks only of personal advantage and is actually exploiting the uneducated.

Commercial television is an example of this. Television advertising is largely aimed at the uneducated. Confidence men and swindlers find innumerable ways to extort money from the ignorant. But the silence of intellectuals who know that many of our laws are unfair because they favor the rich and are made by them is even more inexcusable than the schemes of con men, for those who are well off and educated have an obligation to help the less fortunate. Their silence in the face of injustice makes them the accomplices of those who perpetuate injustice.

The story of Jonah in the Bible points out the responsibility of those who have the gift of words, or the spiritual spark. "The word of the Lord came unto Jonah, the son of Amitai, saying: 'Arise, go to Nineveh, that great city, and cry against it, for their wickedness is come before me.' " Jonah was reluctant to speak out against the wicked of Nineveh. Today, many educated people are equally reluctant to expose injustice, and their failure to speak up allows the powerful to exploit the masses. The ignorant can be intimidated, or even bribed to support laws which are injurious to them.

EVIL BRINGS ITS OWN PUNISHMENT

It is a truism to say that virtue is its own reward, but it is less often stressed that the perpetration of evil never goes unpunished. It is possible to get away with murder, as the saying goes, to escape the legal consequences of one's evil deeds, but the evildoer pays by living on the margin of society, as it were. Morally, he isolates himself from other people. He fears exposure and guards himself against it. If he has any conscience, he suffers from mental anguish. He lives in a prison that he himself has created. Often he is hounded by the police and eventually caught; or, weary of hiding, he gives himself up. Criminals and other wrongdoers can never find true contentment.

Greek mythology speaks of the Furies (Erynnies), avenging goddesses who torment perpetrators of unpunished crimes. The Erynnies are real: they haunt the criminal. And he is alienated from other men even though he dwells among them.

EXPLOITATION

Exploitation occurs when people take advantage of circumstances which allow them to withhold from others money, goods or privileges to which they are entitled. Exploitation is the ugliest and most blatant of human vices; it is also the most widespread, both in individuals and in nations—and has been, throughout human history. Civilization, as we know it today,

137

is largely the result of this exploitation; it is a fact that strong, highly industrialized nations have taken advantage of weaker, more backward states.

Exploitation is the result of ingenuity. Man is desirous of finding help in his struggle against the hardships of life. He first invents tools and machines to that end, and then, given favorable circumstances, prevails upon his fellow creatures, to serve his purposes. Exploitation can take many forms, from the subtlest to the crudest. Here are some examples: the clever salesman who persuades a semi-illiterate to buy a car or a house which he can't really afford, knowing that, in the end, the car or the house will be repossessed by the seller; thus he exploits both the buyer and the seller, deceiving them in order to get his commission. The advertiser who claims his merchandise has qualities which it does not possess, exploits the trust or gullibility of the buyer; the con man who invents schemes to extort money from the unwary; the employer who profits from the immigrant's need for work and pays him starvation wages; the landowner who keeps his farm workers in poverty, so they will agree to work long hours; the owners of sweat shops where the workers toil day and night to eke out a small living; all who prey on the needy are part of an immense army of exploiters. We condemn exploitation as morally wrong, but we actually condone the colossal and continual exploitation of the peoples in the Third World. We buy their raw materials cheaply and sell the finished products at high prices, so that their economic situation, far from improving, is getting worse every year.

Defenseless people are an attractive prey to exploiters. Their defenselessness has been exploited in a particularly revolting way by modern pirates who prey on boat people, those desperate enough to abandon their homes and risk the perils of the sea in small boats in an attempt to find some place to start a new life. Thousands fled from Vietnam in this way, taking what they could with them. Many reached Thailand, where they were interned in refugee camps. Now, however, Thai fishermen

138

regard these people as prey, more lucrative than catching fish. They seize their boats, rape their women, rob the people of everything valuable, and murder them—men, women and children. That they mutilate their victims is revealed by headless corpses which wash ashore. The Thai government has been very lax in ferreting out and arresting such criminals, because they prevent further congestion in refugee camps. Prompted by criticism from other nations, Thailand has set up an anti-piracy expedition which has not yet caught a single pirate.

Haitians also resort to boats to flee their country because they are exploited, condemned to hopeless misery by a corrupt and oppressive government. They, too, become the victims of pirates.

These two particularly loathsome and savage examples affirm the old truth that helplessness invites exploitation. The sadism of these Thai fishermen, if analyzed, could be attributed to their innate bestiality unleashed in a situation where their victims were completely at their mercy. Nazi sadism could be explained the same way.

Power is coveted by many, individuals and governments alike, Man must subordinate himself to the laws of society, but he dreams, consciously or unconsciously, of freeing himself from such restraints. German and Japanese leaders illustrated this naked lust for power. Their writings testify that, had they been victorious, they would have enslaved the world.

Society, though it fights crime, is often guilty of generating it. The law forbids people to steal, but the hungry, unemployed and destitute people see the cards stacked against them. Poverty does not necessarily lead to crime, but can easily engender violence or defiance of the law. The riots in black neighborhoods in the United States in the 60s, characterized by burnings, lootings and destruction, illustrate this fact. Flagrant injustice in verdicts of the courts, inspired by bias against a certain segment of the population, has the same effect. Again we refer to riots of blacks whenever they believed that a crime committed against one of them remained unpunished, or when the perpetrators got away with a too lenient punishment.

Crimes are not committed by the poor alone. Rich people are also tempted to commit crimes in order to increase their wealth. Such a motive is particularly contemptible.

Ignorance of the consequences of getting involved in criminal activity is another factor on the side of evil. People can be talked into doing something illegal and unwittingly become accessories to a crime. Criminal acts are also prompted at times by passion, by hatred or unrequited love. It is interesting to note that the French courts usually show themselves lenient when judging what is termed "crimes passionels," admitting mitigating circumstances.

Crimes will never be completely eliminated, but it is undeniable that those committed by individuals can, in the final analysis, be explained in most cases by unjust laws and institutions. Great inequality engenders feelings of rebellion, which in turn breed criminal acts.

GOOD MUST BECOME AN ABSOLUTE VALUE

In spite or because of the ambivalence in human nature, good *must* be defined in absolute terms, otherwise mankind will destroy itself. If Pascal's notion that what is good on this side of the Pyrenees might be considered evil on the other side should prevail in international relations, there would be no basis on which one could find an agreement to prevent a worldwide holocaust.

There have been constant attempts to codify the rules by which all nations should be bound in their behavior toward each other. The terrible aftermath of World War I made people aware of the need to prevent wars. The League of Nations was founded, followed in 1927 by the Kellogg-Briand Pact, whose signatories, some 15 nations, pledged never to resort to war as

140

an instrument of national policy. The signatories included Germany and the United States.

The League had no power to punish aggressor nations, so that Germany and Italy could with impunity launch the conquests which provoked a new international conflict, more devastating than World War I. This second world war left the European continent in ruins and cost the lives of many millions. The United Nations has also failed to secure "pacem in terris," peace among men, mainly because of the rivalry between the Soviet Union and the United States, but also because of the economic polarization of peoples into haves and have-nots.

Since World War II there has always been conflict somewhere, but war between the major powers has been prevented by our terror of nuclear weapons. One wonders how long this deterrent will be effective. All nations, rich or poor, are impoverished because of the enormous sums spent on defense. Are we more secure for possessing all these lethal and sophisticated weapons? Actually we are less secure, because our potential adversaries are also arming at a frenetic rate, so that both sides must continue until they are completely exhausted or until one or the other, in a panic, sends out a missile. The result of such an action is too horrible to contemplate.

This misuse of their resources leads nations to neglect the legitimate needs of their people. Within every nation there is increasing hostility between haves and have-nots, which breeds anarchy. Religious and national fanaticism also foster violence; terrorists of various brands unite to form an international gang, ready to commit any crime. The original reason why these terrorists have exiled themselves from society is often lost sight of, and only the will to destroy remains. Thus, human civilization, a degree of modus vivendi among the peoples of the earth, is gradually undermined, heralding a new dark age. With it may come unprecedented destruction.

The atrocities which we have already outlined give us a foretaste of things to come. There is no escape from global destruction, not on earth and not in space either, for its conquest is also part of the preparation for the next war.

We know very well that there is only one remedy for this state of affairs; we must reform ourselves and cultivate integrity in both personal and international relations. Humanity must face the fact that adherence to standards of morality, preached by religions and philosophers, is its only hope of salvation. This is no longer the goal of a dreamy utopia, but an ineluctable necessity.

The sober appraisal of choices and their consequences sometimes impels a moral act. Slavery eventually was abolished in the United States when the highly industrialized North found it more economical to employ wage slaves than to buy Negroes. Employees could always be laid off if they failed to earn their keep. The awareness that slavery was morally wrong came later. Similarly, we ought to realize that the armament race leads to sure economic ruin and chaos in the world, that there is no safety in it, and that it is likely to result in a war from which we would never recover.

A LAST WORD ON MORALITY

Meditations, dissertations on good and evil seem futile in view of the crude reality as regards morality in the world today. Two world wars, the resulting economic and political upheaval, and continuous smaller wars in our century brought to the surface in human beings the savage instincts that had been repressed by the efforts of civilization. As killings are practiced, prepared and organized by nations, tribes, groups and individuals against real, potential or imagined enemies, the sane commandment "Thou shalt not kill!" is discarded, nay, mocked at.

Killing has become an instrument of policy, routine in the power struggle that pits nations against nations, religious groups against other religious groups, opponents of any kind against each other. Terrorism is rampant all over the world. Torture of prisoners, imprisonment without trial, putting dissenters in forced labor camps, in mental institutions, replace

142

the principles devised to protect the individual from arbitrariness.

The savage practices described here are not the monopoly of a single nation. They exist among the most civilized countries. Those in power know no restraint in abusing their defenseless opponents. The moral code that has held the nations together is ignored. The human condition has become more precarious. It is today dangerous to live in society, dangerous to live alone. The voice of the philosopher, of the humanist, of the preachers of human solidarity is today a voice in the wilderness, and this wilderness is human society.

Does this mean that this voice should be muted, that the upholders of morality should remain silent? On the contrary. Prophets are most necessary when they are not listened to. Ultimately their voice will prevail, because it is the voice of life against the forces of destruction.

The world today is sick, but this sickness is not incurable. And the idealists who have not ceased to believe in the victory of the good are the real realists, because cynicism about human nature carries its own defeat. Man will overcome his instinct of self-destruction because mankind deserves to survive. And survival is only possible when human societies rest on solid moral foundations.

Chapter VI

COSMIC TRINITY AND COSMIC DUALITY

In a previous chapter, we quoted this line from the philosopher-poet Lucretius: "The universe is formed of a mortal body and at the same time it had birth." And Aristotle speculated that everything, except the First Mover, is constantly changing; that is, everything is perishing and constantly being renewed.

These two philosophers of Greek and Roman antiquity enunciated the *two fundamental laws that govern all creation:* the Law of Cosmic Trinity and the Law of Cosmic Duality, without, however, pointing out their interrelationship and the deep significance and wisdom of it.

The Law of Cosmic Trinity determines that everything on earth, and Earth itself, our solar system and all the galaxies, everything, in fact, that is, had birth, is developing and will have an end. The Law of Cosmic Duality ordains that every creature shall conform to the general pattern of its own kind and yet have individual characteristics, making it distinct from every other.

In Greek mythology, the laws of Cosmic Trinity and Cosmic Duality are symbolized by the three Fates. Clotho spins the thread of human life, Lachesis furnishes the yarn, and Atropos cuts it. Their action is incessant, inexorable.

The Law of Cosmic Trinity is everywhere apparent. We see the newborn babe progress to youth and middle age, and finally to dissolution. We witness one by one the deaths of those we know or hear of. Around us trees and plants are growing and decaying, flowers blossoming and withering. Astronomy confirms the gradual cooling of stars; we hear of black holes, dead stars so dense that even light cannot get through them. Death

144

is present everywhere and so is birth; the two are complementary. Reflection tells us that one is necessary for the other, that life could not exist without death. Life would be impossible without death, because of overcrowding, because eternal life would be permanent stagnation, an obstacle to renewal.

Cosmic duality—the fact that each belongs to a definite species yet is different in some way from every other in that category—is also clear to us. We are all members of the human species, yet we are individual. Generally speaking, we are prone to see members of other races as all alike. But if we get to know more than one Chinese person, for instance, or travel to a Chinese city, then we become aware of the difference between individuals. This must be true of all creation. Every tree, nay, every leaf, is different from all others, as every grain of sand and every microbe, though we may not perceive this with the naked eye.

The two laws, the Law of Cosmic Trinity and the Law of Cosmic Duality, annul—and at the same time confirm—each other. This interlinking of the two laws makes up the ever active, ever valid, efficient process of creation.

THE TWO LAWS:
PROOF OF THE CREATIVE INTELLIGENCE OF THE UNIVERSE

The end of all life and the eternal renewal of life are proof that intelligence governs the universe. The two laws, that determine life, death and the renewal of life, constitute the essence of the plan that underlies all creation. We cannot in human language characterize the wisdom and validity of these two laws—speaking of the plan, we can only use the inadequate word "perfection."

COSMIC DUALITY: FREEDOM AND SELECTION

All creatures are fated to die, but each is born different from all others and is endowed with the ability and the freedom to develop his individual potential. The creative play of nature is comparable to a dramatic production in which each character comes on, says what he has to say, and disappears. Or, to use another metaphor, the harmonies of creation are like the movement of a symphony in which one leitmotiv runs throughout. The Law of Cosmic Duality assures growth and progress in nature. But the freedom it allows us entails strife and competition, the struggle for survival. Nothing stagnates, for this turmoil is continual in nature.

FREEDOM IS LIMITED BY THE NEED OF THE COLLECTIVITY

Human freedom must be limited to ensure safety. Where freedom is not limited, there is insecurity. Freedom limited is freedom strengthened. Without restriction of freedom, anyone can attack me, rob me of my property, and many will do so if they can get away with it. Everyone must be his brother's keeper, and guard his neighbor's freedom as he does his own. This is self-evident, yet so many of us still do not understand it or do not want to understand it.

Fortunately, there are still "impractical idealists," who understand this truth and try to implement it by their deeds. A man by the name of Mitch Snyder fasted 51 days to force the American administration under President Reagan to remodel an old Federal building to give shelter to some thousand homeless people. He won. The President consented after long negotiations. This man's action matched Saint Kolbe's. People like them are true heroes, modern redeemers of humanity. This sinful world, full of selfishness, of ugly, evil deeds, would perish without such personal demonstrations on belief in human solidarity. Because of them, this ideal ceases to be hollow; therefore, it becomes emphatic reality.

FREEDOM IS CHANCE UNPREDICTABILITY

The freedom which each individual enjoys in nature gives every man an opportunity to invent something that will give him or his group certain advantages in the struggle for survival. This freedom entails the operation of another law which prevails in nature, namely *unpredictability*. Unpredictability is a corollary to freedom; it is another aspect of the master plan, another manifestation of the Creative Intelligence of the Universe.

Causality is not annulled by unpredictability: though the cause is willed, its effect on the individual is unforeseeable. If a small fish swims in a certain direction, a big fish might be close enough to devour it. Should a certain individual or individuals hit upon a new idea in the course of their development, the result might be a new variety of the species, or what we call mutation—a completely unexpected result.

Chance, accident are other names for the unpredictability that rules all life. Why is one born with a high degree of intelligence, while another has only a limited grasp of things? The original cause is given in both cases; one can point to heredity and other factors, but as far as the individual is concerned, this is simply a case of good luck or bad luck.

Why is there life on our planet, and none on other planets in our solar system? The answer that life arose here because certain requirements for its formation were present, states the cause for a process (the formation of life) but it was nevertheless an accident that those requirements happened to exist on earth rather than on Jupiter. A plane crashes; two hundred people die, one person survives. Why? To be sure, there is a cause: he or she happened to be seated in a place in the plane which felt the impact of the crash least, or due to some other factors. Whatever they were, you would call that person lucky, wouldn't you?

Unpredictability is the inevitable consequence of freedom, though at first it may seem contrary to it. Freedom gives us a chance to invent, to change. If everything were predictable, there would be no choice, no freedom. There is no providence, there is only freedom and chance, good and bad luck, the opportunity to act on impulse or to plan. Planning itself is subject to the unpredictable. Chance entails risk, but risk is an ingredient of freedom.

In human life one encounters the unexpected at every step. There are natural disasters, such as earthquake and flood, loss of loved ones, or financial losses, accidents of all sorts. Events such as these may radically alter our lives. They can influence our thinking, so the problem for us is to preserve our self-determination in any situation. Our freedom is within us and should enable us to dominate our circumstances. Epictetus was a slave, yet retained an equanimity within, which made him a freer man than the master who abused him. We must claim for ourselves the preestablished harmony of which Leibniz spoke.

To maintain such self-possession is the most important challenge in life, and should be the aim of human existence. If we succeed in establishing harmony within ourselves, we shall triumph over chance and what is unpredictable. Outside events will not disturb us. We shall be in harmony with the universal law that wills eternal change to assure the renewal of the quality of life. This is what is called peace of mind, serenity. We shall not fear what is to come, but welcome the unforeseen as the salt of life. How well we cope with the unexpected will be the measure of our true worth.

The Universe is indeed a marvel, and life wondrously exciting, *because* of change and happenstance. Freedom and unpredictability form thesis and anti-thesis united in synthesis, as Hegel saw it. Freedom and unpredictability enable humans to dream. If everything is possible, man can dream of anything. Fairy tales express human aspirations: they speak of seven-league boots, and we have since invented the airplane with which to overcome distances. The hero of a tale arrives in a country in which time loses its hold on you, and we have now discovered that velocity weakens the effect of time on the traveller; we dream of immortality and extend the human life more and more. We are free to dream and ready to take risks for freedom, like the fairy tale heroes who brave all dangers to reach their goal.

The Law of Cosmic Duality is a law made to the human measure.

THE CREATURE BECOMES CREATOR

By virtue of the Law of Cosmic Duality, the creature becomes creator in its own right. Every creature is infused with the creative spirit of the universe so it can continue, affirm, establish and embellish the work of creation.

The Law of Cosmic Duality guarantees the functioning of life, and also its quality. The creature ceases to be completely dependent upon its creator. This gives it dignity. Having the opportunity to create in its own right leaves the creature free to make choices. Creating is both the result and the culmination of freedom; it is immortality. The Creator lives in its creature, which is a wise and profound arrangement. It applies to the whole universe.

In nature, individual creativity ensures not only the survival, but also the improvement of the species. Spiders weave their webs and all varieties of them learn to weave better and better webs to attract their potential victims. Sea anemones have learned to develop beautiful, flowerlike shapes for the same purpose. Intelligence is expressed in every creature, as it creates, recreates, develops and improves.

The work becoming independent of its master is manifestly true in the domain of art. Hamlet is very much alive, though his creator, Shakespeare, has long been dead. The artist, writer or composer often finds that the work on which he has labored has slipped from his hands and taken a road he had never thought of when he conceived it. Eugene Ionesco, one of the most original of French plyawrights, calls this "the creative mechanism." A symbol of this phenomenon is the Golem, a mystical figure into whose mouth a rabbi placed a magic word that lent him a soul. In our modern world we lend souls to our machines, the computers and robots which we "program." A formula is inserted which they use to perform tasks beyond our own capabilities.

Here on earth man takes over the role of the Universal Creator. This is the task he was created to perform. He must become aware of his purpose and fulfill it. He must not fail. If he does, he will become waste material to be recast by the "Button Molder," a symbolic figure created by Ibsen. This was to have been the fate of Peer Gynt had he not been saved by Solveig's love.

THE LAW OF COSMIC DUALITY EXPLAINS NATURE'S MISTAKES

Nature is like an artist who is striving to express an idea that is important to him and makes numerous sketches to that end. Each of the sketches renders some aspect of his theme, but none satisfies him completely. Some of the sketches turn out to be wholly unsatisfactory, so he throws them away. In human terms, nature's failures may result in children born with some defect—perhaps they are retarded or stillborn. Causality is always there: parents or ancestors have done something that caused the birth defect in their descendants. This is symbolically expressed in the Bible, when God says that He punishes the sins of the parents unto the third and the fourth generations.

Causality, that is, the parent's sins, creates a new determinism for the offspring, reducing their individual freedom. Human science now has some ability to correct nature's mistakes, and in time is certain to have more. Genetic engineering can sometimes remake, or can give the newborn a more nearly normal life. However, it is dangerous to tamper with the Law of Cosmic Duality. The new science of genetics can be used for good or evil. It may destroy the freedom that man has by virtue of the law. It could create a society in which every human being would have his place and would conform to his genetic makeup.

150

In *Brave New World,* Aldous Huxley has given us a grim picture of this kind of planned society—to show us what we may be heading for.

Nature never intends to produce misfits; man has this capability and there is the danger that he will use it.

THE LAW OF COSMIC DUALITY EXPLAINS THE EXISTENCE OF EVIL

Ever since man conceived a God Almighty, he has been baffled by the existence of evil. Why does God allow the oppression of the weak and poor, the exploitation of the defenseless, the murder of innocent women and children? Why does He tolerate this ceaseless human warfare—cities being burned, bombs dropped from the skies? How can He suffer the sight of such terrible things? Why does He not strike down the wicked and wipe out evil on this earth?

The answer people give to such questions is generally a nonanswer: "God knows what He is doing," and similar evasions. Faith acquiesces in what it cannot explain. Reason, however, is not satisfied until it receives an answer it can accept. The Law of Cosmic Duality tells us that, aside from the determinism of birth, deployment and death, freedom reigns in the universe. *The Creator does not interfere in the actions of his creatures!*

Homo sapiens, like any other creature, organizes his own life. The Universal Grand Design is not affected by men's actions. Cosmic laws will continue to obtain whatever humans do. Nature does not concern herself with good and evil: men must do this.

Spinoza said, "God has committed himself to his own law, he has no power to change it." Whitehead emphasized that God is inside nature, and experience constantly reminds us that nature is indifferent to our welfare.

We must conclude that evil is man-made, since the Law of Cosmic Duality makes man free and responsible for his actions. *God is not responsible.* Man makes his own heaven or hell on earth. It is pointless to drag God into it.

The Law of Cosmic Duality spells freedom and unpredictability. If individuals are free, they have a choice of actions. If God (the Supreme Intelligence) knew how they would choose to act, this would annul the law which allows every creature to be individual. Foreknowledge and freedom of action are contradictory.

The contradiction in the basic tenets of Christianity, which professes both the freedom of the individual and the omniscience of God, has deeply troubled Church fathers, theologians and Scholastic philosophers throughout the Middle Ages. Various explanations were offered, but none proved satisfactory. None could reconcile the contradiction.

The awareness of the Law of Cosmic Duality gives us the answer. The Law spells freedom—freedom that makes every individual a creator, and cannot and will not determine what free individuals will or will not do. A predetermined universe is incompatible with the creative intelligence bestowed on every creature. The opposite would result in a stagnant universe, incapable of development because development requires freedom of action. Life, instead of having its present kaleidoscopic diversity, would be reduced to a monotonous routine. Life would lose all meaning, creation would be an empty mechanism, and all creatures puppets. The puppets would be mindless, for they would have no need of intelligence.

God is not omniscient because he wants all creatures to be free.

PRAYER WILL NOT HELP

If man is free and God does not interfere with his life, he cannot escape nor elude his responsibility by asking God to change what he or someone else has done. It is not that easy. Just let us consider: if God dwelling in Heaven were accessible to all the beseeching words addressed to him from every part of this planet, and if he were a God who could be swayed by human desire, he would be a wishy-washy God, indeed. What would happen to his master plan if he were to change his mind at the request of every Tom, Dick and Harry? And surely, prayers addressed to him are often contradictory. During the mass murder which erring, foolish man calls war, prayers are sent up by the opposite nations, each asking him to bless their cause. Whose prayers will he heed?

We must remember that God does not interfere in human affairs. We ourselves must take care of these; we must resolve our own problems.

Prayers have been traveling through the waves every second of every day ever since humans conceived of superior powers. We pointed out in the Introduction the various means by which man has tried to propitiate (a better word is "to bribe") these powers. The attempt to induce God to meet our demands is inseparably linked to an anthropomorphic concept of the divinity. Those who see God as manlike naturally suppose that he can be persuaded to change his mind. The ancient Hebrews believed God was their ally against all other nations.

Sometimes the value of prayer is its potential for autosuggestion. The French autosuggestionist, Emile Coué, treated his patients by such a method, telling them to repeat every morning: "I feel better and better."

The Christian Science practitioner proceeds in a different way. He does not send prayers skyward, for he knows that God is everywhere. He seeks to realize the ever-presence of harmony and the unreality of discord. While the medical profession has classified many diseases as psychosomatic, Christian Science believes that all disease is an aberration of the human mind. This belief ignores the Law of Cosmic Trinity, which postulates that all that is born must decay and perish. And a virus infecting some of our organs is not an aberration of our mind, but a fact independent of our mind. Hepatitis, hardening of the arteries, diabetes and innumerable other diseases can affect

153

anyone, no matter how well adjusted, how mentally healthy he is. History is full of examples of bodily diseased people known for their powerful, noble or systematic thinking. The Agnostic concedes the right to approach the art of healing in more than one way. Mental healing is one of these ways. However, he rejects the claim that all disease is but a disorder of the mind as preposterous and deceptive. Such a claim is liable to induce people to renounce traditional medical care, for the lack of which they might die. The Agnostic believes that man must be the maker of his own miracles.

Chapter VII

THE CREED OF AN AGNOSTIC

INTRODUCTION

Agnosticism is also faith—faith in the creative process, the constant renewal, which is the work of Supreme Intelligence. Faith in the all-pervading spirit, which the Greeks called Nous, which Giordano Bruno perceived and refused to deny, though he must die for it. Faith also in Man, in his ability to make life on earth a continuous renewal, an ever varying harmony, his own creation and worthy of his genius.

The Agnostic urges man to work at this task tirelessly. He believes that working for the good of mankind makes human life meaningful. He means good in the absolute sense. One cannot disagree with Pascal when he extols the marvels of creation, both the infinitely vast and the infinitely small. One cannot but share the wonder of Leibniz, who discovered that the design and operation of everything, and every part of everything, from the microscopic to the infinitely vast constellations, are identical. What one sees through the telescope and the microscope testifies to the intelligence that governs the universe. Life's mechanism, both the defense for survival and the securing of life's needs, requires intelligence that is constantly on the alert. The spider and sea anemone, the orchid and the cactuses, as well as countless other creatures, all know instinctively how to secure their food, how to assure the survival of their species. The very word "life" is inseparably linked to the word "intelligence." The variety of ways in which this intelligence manifests itself, and the ingenuity of it, are so astounding that we must conclude that a Supreme Intelligence is constantly at work in all things and creatures to produce this miracle.

Religions profess that the Creator is outside of his creation. The Agnostic says: "All we know is that nature is replete with the creative spirit. Let us give ourselves to the job of being part of it." In his tragedy, *The Trojan Women,* Euripides makes one of his characters exclaim: "Whoever you are, O Zeus, you are hard to espy, necessity of nature or spirit of man, to you I cry!"

This statement perfectly expresses the Agnostic's feeling. We shall never apprehend the whole of creation, but this is no reason for giving up our efforts to learn more. On the contrary: the Agnostic is convinced that the deeper we penetrate the wisdom of the Great Design, the more joy and reverence we shall experience.

SCIENCE VERSUS RELIGION

Science progresses, religion does not. Each step in scientific progress modifies or amplifies former theories. Every scientist knows that the discoveries he has made, the theories he has elaborated, will be superseded by newer discoveries, newer theories. Scientific findings are always subject to criticism, to re-evaluation. This is a needed challenge to the searching mind. If there were nothing more to discover, why should we be here? In science there are no dogmas; if a theory proves to be incorrect, if it does not correspond to newer discoveries, the scientific mind abandons it, no matter how well entrenched the theory has been. Euclidian geometry was the whole of our geometrical knowledge until the 19th century, when it was discovered that other geometrical systems were also possible; we now know that there are cases in which Euclidian theorems do not apply.

Science must be tolerant of dissent. Religion proclaims eternal truths; it cannot tolerate what it calls heresy. Science thrives on it; heresy makes it exciting and stimulating. In spite of the rigidity of religious dogmas, heresies keep springing up in every religion. At the time of this writing, in the fall of 1984, Iran and Iraq are waging a savage war against each other. The issue of the war on the part of Iraq is territory; on the part of Iran it is religion. The Iranian religious leader, Ayatollah Khomeini, wants to overthrow the regime in Iraq so he can establish a government composed of Muslims of his own denomination.

The Agnostic, who does not claim to know the truth, will always be open-minded. He never forgets that he is part of the universe and that the part is unable to comprehend the whole.

Religion belittles man so as to glorify God. For the Agnostic, the word "God" is a vague term. He only knows that there is intelligence in the universe—that intelligence is life and creation. He knows that man has greater intelligence than any other creature on this planet. The Agnostic extolls man in this sense, as the king of our planet by virtue of the creative intelligence with which he is endowed.

Saint Augustine and more modern religious philosophers, such as Martin Buber, Richard Niebuhr, and others, emphasize that human conduct, human ethics must be judged according to religious revelation. The Agnostic conducts his life according to his own conscience, and he is the sternest judge of his own ethics.

Religion is a safe haven where people install themselves comfortably. God takes care of them and they take care of God by observing the rites of a particular religion. Religion does not encourage questions, but rather compliance, whereas the right to question is the Agnostic's most precious freedom.

Saint Augustine and Pascal, who were Roman Catholics, believed in their dogmas, albeit, or rather *because* they were absurd (credo *quia* absurdum). The Agnostic understands that one can believe something even though it looks absurd on the surface, but he cannot see how one can believe in something *because* of its absurdity. Such a statement seems to him the peak of absurdity. The Agnostic believes that there is planning in the universe, just as Christians do; he does not believe, though, that this plan excludes fortuitous events, chance or accidents, but rather that it postulates them. This is a cardinal

157

tenet of the creed of the Agnostic: there is freedom within determinism by virtue of the laws of Cosmic Trinity and Cosmic Duality. A tree, a volcano, or a worm plays a certain role in the scheme of things, but each owes its existence to evolution which is independent of the overall concept of the Cosmos. This overall concept makes allowance for the chance emergence of trees, volcanoes or worms. The laws of Cosmic Trinity and of Cosmic Duality provide the framework, and there is freedom for the individual within that framework. The tree is free to adjust to its location and climate, finding a way to get enough sun or moisture. The business of living is adjustment to the conditions of life; *adjustment is creativeness.* Adjustment is evolution, and life is evolution.

Creativeness is opposed to mere existence. Human life has meaning to the extent that the individual is emerging from, rather then just merging with, the common run of humanity.

ALL CREATURES ARE FELLOWS

Biology teaches us that "homo sapiens" differ from animals not in the quality, but the size of his brain. The Agnostic is humble and grateful that he has received a greater share of the creative spirit than members of other species. He realizes, however, that all creatures are subject to the same laws and to the same cosmic destiny. He looks upon animals as fellow creatures. Like Saint Francis, he calls the birds "my brethren."

Loving all creatures brings him closer to his fellow men. He says with Martin Buber, the Jewish philosopher, "I am Thou." This one short sentence summarizes the teachings of all evolved religions, of all philosophies. Because he identifies himself with all human beings, the Agnostic does everything in his power to increase the well-being of all. He supports any cause which promotes justice, knowing that equity promotes prosperity and freedom. To the Agnostic, freedom is the magic word It is his guiding star. Freedom may also be likened to a cornucopia, a

158

horn of plenty, which contains all that makes life worth living. We must have freedom from injustice of any kind, economic, social, or political. We also need freedom of choice, freedom from indoctrination and freedom of inquiry; we must be able to see things uninhibited by the shackles of authority, of tradition. It is also imperative that physical and social sciences should work to eliminate human suffering, insofar as this is possible. Above all, we must have freedom from war, which could instantly abolish all human progress, or even wipe out humanity itself.

The Agnostic devotes his life to combating those forces which obstruct human freedom. This is his noblest contribution to humanity in this imperfect world.

THE AGNOSTIC AND THE ATHEIST

Cardinal Newman, in his work *The Idea of a University,* quoted by William James, declares: "I do not see much difference avowing that there is no God and implying that nothing can be known for certain about him." This is a presumptuous statement, typical of a religious fanatic. In reality, nothing can be further from the Agnostic than atheism. To declare that God does not exist is just as void of meaning for the Agnostic as the attitude of the religionists who know God inside out, talk to him, read his mind, invoke him on all occasions, attribute to the Supreme Being their own vile or petty thoughts and impulses, arm themselves with the authority of God to camouflage their often deceitful designs.

The Law of Cosmic Duality teaches the Agnostic that he alone is responsible for what he does or fails to do. His actions must prove the value of his individual contribution. It is unfair to accuse the Agnostic of maintaining that all is without purpose. He who perceives that he is endowed with intelligence necessarily concludes that this intelligence is intended to be used. This is a sufficient reason for the Agnostic; it fills him with a sense of responsibility.

It is a sufficient reason to elevate his thoughts without constructing myths or building churches. This is a sufficient reason for the Agnostic to feel one with all creatures. He does not choose, as so many do, to confine himself to a particular belief, keeping out, or even quarreling with, those who do not share it.

The atheist bases his belief on the absence of proof that God exists. He does not see that proof in the laws of physics, the laws which govern the stars and galaxies, as well as every living being. He does not see in these phenomena a plan or great design. To him it is all an accident, whereas Agnostics conclude that the Laws of Cosmic Trinity and Cosmic Duality account both for order and chance in the universe. The universe, we repeat, operates within a determined framework—the iron law of Cosmic Trinity, which nevertheless allows for freedom, unpredictability, and chance.

The fundamental difference between the atheist and the agnostic is that the agnostic does not deny, does not doubt the existence of God, but declares him to be unknowable, or that which surpasses human intelligence. The atheist might or might not feel an obligation to society. If there is no God, then no intelligence dictates the movements of the universe and man is free of any obligation. He is a law unto himself.

This amorality led to the concept of the Superman and the Super Race, the fatal consequences of which were clearly manifested during the Second World War. The Superman theory cynically ignores the respect due to every human being because of the cosmic intelligence of which he partakes. It is based entirely on a power relationship: might is right. It is abhorrent to an agnostic.

An agnostic must be of progressive mind; he will take nothing for granted. He must examine every statement, from whatever quarter, and any question, seeking to test its validity. Agnosticism restores man's dignity, for in freeing himself from any particular religion, man becomes the carrier, upholder and standard-bearer of the Universal Spirit, representative on

160

earth of the highest intelligence—an independent creator, not merely a creature in the hands, or at the mercy of, God.

PANTHEISM AND THE UNCREATED

A Creator who has never been created but has always been is a concept which the human mind cannot grasp. It runs counter to the Law of Cosmic Trinity, which postulates that everything which exists was born and must perish. Plato's and Aristotle's conclusion that logic must admit the existence of a Prime Mover remains an abstraction to which nothing corresponds in our reality, a concept which cannot be proven unless we take the so-called revelations of the various religions at their face value.

Pantheism associates the idea of the Uncreated with the universe—not necessarily with this universe, but with *a* universe, because the universe has always existed in some form. On the face of it, this answer seems satisfactory. But it does not answer the question: Who conceived this great design, this idea of a self-renewing universe?

All matter is but the representation of an idea. In the beginning there was the idea. If the celestial bodies were formed by accident, as a result of a concourse of circumstances, that concourse of circumstances itself must have been the effect of some cause; otherwise, we must abstract the Creative Intelligence which pervades the whole universe. If this intelligence was responsible for the conditions which resulted in the formation of celestial bodies, we are back to the Prime Mover. One can see nothing, perceive nothing outside of Cosmos. A Creator who directs the universe from outside raises the question: Where is that outside, if it is not in the Cosmos?

The enigma of the Prime Mover will remain an enigma; neither pantheism nor science can offer a satisfactory answer. Science will discover more and more about the secrets of the universe, but will not learn anything about the Uncreated.

Science is concerned about the *What,* not about the *Why.* Man must concentrate his efforts on goals within his reach, not lose himself in the jungle of metaphysical enigmas.

MAN MUST STAND ON HIS OWN FEET

The Law of Cosmic Duality accounts for the fact that man is alone with nature, with his society, with himself. This is the iron law which man has been trying to evade ever since he learned to think, although nature's indifference to human well-being stares man in the face. We find it hard to resign ourselves, so we have invented gods—and finally a single God who, we hope, will help us. It is illogical to conceive of him as immutable and yet accessible to our supplications.

We do not wish to see the contradiction in this concept of God. If God could be induced by prayer to change his mind, what kind of an unstable, capricious God would he be? What kind of a universe would we have? How could man rely on the wisdom of his decisions? Should we not be afraid that, if our adversaries prayed more eloquently, he would change his mind again?

Despite the evidence, man refuses to realize that he is on his own, that he can count on no metaphysical partner in the adventure of life. He clings to his illusion as a consolation. God is a crutch for the child-man who is afraid of walking without help. Pascal speaks about the misery of man without God. He is right. Man needs God to shield him from the perils of existence, against his own anxiety, against the fear of death.

People may take the Agnostic to task, telling him: "Why do you want to deprive people of the hope that turning to their Father in Heaven offers? Are those who no longer pray happier for it?" No, they are not, though it is not proven that life without prayer is necessarily an unhappy one. Generations are growing up all over the world who have never prayed, never been ex-

162

posed to prayer or have ceased to pray. They have, as far as is known, no more than the usual number of frustrations. The absence of prayer is not necessarily a contributing factor.

That, however, is beside the point. The Agnostic speaks out, as does the scientist when he makes a discovery—regardless of its implications. Atomic energy was discovered and used to manufacture the bomb and other frightful atomic weapons; it could, however, also be used for purposes that would greatly benefit humanity. Intelligence illuminates hitherto obscure corners of the knowable; it is up to us to use the things that are found there to help mankind.

The discoverer is not responsible. Some scientific discoveries were inevitable as a result of simultaneous efforts made in different countries. Truth remains truth, and it is man's choice and responsibility to decide what he does with it. The Agnostic knows that in proclaiming the inefficacy of prayer, he may meet with the hostility of those who make a living out of it. He may also be resented by many who find solace and reassurance in prayer. Yet he believes that he who has recognized the truth must proclaim it. The Agnostic is aware that the incantations of prayer will continue to hypnotize the millions who do not dare to look the truth in the face and prefer to live in illusions. The world of make-believe is a warm, cozy house where it is good to dwell; reality is outside, an unknown world that frightens us. Nevertheless, as mankind grows up, it will realize that the intelligence humans have received from nature obliges them to do better than waste it on illusion. It is incumbent upon humans to be found worthy of this unique gift of nature.

THE IMMORTALITY OF THE SOUL

The word "soul" corresponds to nothing tangible, nothing that can be experienced. Its meaning is undefined; at times it is equated with the heart in a figurative sense. We say "he (or

163

she) is a good soul," meaning a good-hearted person. American blacks call each other "soul brothers," that is, people expressing racial solidarity in a white world. At other times, "soul" is synonymous with a human being: "There was not a soul around."

In religious terms, the word represents what is believed to be the immortal part of man—that which survives the death of the body. This belief, that humans have an immortal essence, has been prevalent since ancient times. Among the Egyptians, as well as among the Greeks and Romans, soul has been conceived of as an ethereal substance, like breath or ether, a species of fire. The ancient Egyptians believed that the soul will return to the body in which it was housed; that is why they embalmed the bodies of the dead and laid into their tombs all the objects which the dead person had used in his lifetime. The belief in the survival of the soul after death prompted the construction of the pyramids and was an inspiration to the arts.

The ancient Hebrews conceived of the soul as the equivalent of the principle of life as embodied in living creatures, and this meaning continued throughout the Bible.

We have already spoken of the Buddhist belief in the migration of the soul; this doctrine clearly conceives of the soul as equivalent to human consciousness. If it is reborn in an animal, it feels the agony and pain of degradation. Souls are judged after they separate from the body in most evolved religions. In fairy tales, the soul is often the symbol of life, as in Hebrew mythology. It can be hidden somewhere and, as long as it remains intact, the owner of the soul is immune to attacks from his enemies.

If we apply the criterion of reason to the belief in the survival of the soul, one must remain utterly skeptical of the doctrine. Assuming that the soul enters the body at the latter's birth, what happens to it in the case of a newborn child who dies after a few minutes of its coming into the world? What about the test-tube babies, when a fertilized egg is implanted into the mother's womb? And has the fetus already a soul? What

164

happens to the soul of Siamese twins separated by surgical intervention? Which of the twins will receive a soul, or were they endowed with two souls after birth? What souls have received morons, idiots, freaks of all sorts?

A realistic view of biological life shows that humans are subject to the same natural conditions as other creatures. They die, and that is the end of their story. They survive in the memory of those who have known them and on whose lives they have had an impact. A teacher's immortality is in the memory of his former students; an artist's in the work he has created. Any person's immortality exists as long as people remember that person. This is beautifully symbolized in a play, *The Bluebird,* by the Belgian author Maurice Maeterlinck. Two children are searching for the bluebird of happiness and, in the course of their peregrinations, they remember their grandparents. The latter immediately awaken in their graves. Those who are remembered never die completely.

If we identify the soul with the spirit that creates life, then all creatures, animals, plants, even minerals have a soul, as professed by Giordano Bruno. Either everything has a soul or nothing has. The experience of life teaches us that creatures, dead, have ceased to exist. André Gide wrote in his diary (entry of September 15, 1941): "It is more than difficult for me to imagine that the soul may prolong its existence beyond the death of the body."

To the Agnostic,the death of the body indicates that the All-Animating Spirit which has given part of itself to that particular individual during his lifetime will now cease to do so. Reason tells the Agnostic that this individual "soul" vanishes with the body. It must be so, because life is evolution. The Creative Spirit of the Universe will develop ever more perfect intelligences. It has no use for the old ones. Why should any John Doe survive when new, more perfect John Does are being prepared in the kitchen of the Great Chef? The life of any individual has an actual, as well as a symbolic significance. Each life makes a statement. I, John Doe, have lived and made my statement. Now I must make room for others.

165

The immortality of the soul is another catchy slogan, by which we humans try to mitigate the terror of death. Religion, as we have said, has seized upon this hope, a brilliant feather in its cap. However, in abstract terms, immortality runs counter to the Law of Cosmic Trinity, which has decreed that all life, except Life itself, (that is, the Creative Spirit of the Universe) must come to an end.

The Agnostic does not live in terror of Hell, nor in expectation of heavenly bliss. He builds his immortality in this life, every moment.

THE AGNOSTIC AND THE CHRISTIAN

The Agnostic will walk hand in hand with the Christian in what is called the Christian way of life, which in popular parlance means to be law-abiding, to be ready to help one's neighbor and to have compassion for the unfortunate. Obviously, he will not go to church, because he believes the clergy deals in nothing but mirage and illusions. God does not enter into his scheme of things because he cannot resort to the easy subterfuge of creating him in his own image, as many Christians do.

Aware of the Law of Cosmic Duality which determines that each individual is free within the limitations of Cosmic destiny, he will seek the underlying cause of all events, point out the sources of evil, and fight evil with all the means at his disposal.

The Agnostic, like the Christian, will resort to what the philosopher David Hume called "the foremost quality of the human mind," namely self-abstraction. Self-abstraction is the ability of being subject and object at the same time, to regard oneself as another person, judged by your other self. He will not, as Christians do, display his sins publicly in the certainty that the priest will absolve him, provided he complies with the penance imposed upon him. The self-examination of the Agnostic aims at self-knowledge. He will try by this process to banish vanity from his mind, to arrive at a proper estimate of his place and potential in the world. This process is a kind of Agnostic form of existentialism which will help him decide what goals he should strive for.

Recognizing the freedom that is granted to all creatures by virtue of the Law of Cosmic Duality, the Agnostic is aware of the possibility of chance, of luck and misfortune in human affairs. Their existence greatly contributes to the interest in and excitement of life. Still, the Agnostic suspects that behind luck or misfortune there may be human meddling or human malice. The Agnostic refuses to toss everything, good and evil, into the lap of God, declaring that it was God's will. He has but contempt, mixed with commiseration for the fundamentalist, who lets his child die rather than call a doctor because he distrusts worldly science. The Agnostic rejects outright the Christian belief that only those who are baptized can enter Paradise. Though Paradise is, as we have said, a mirage to the Agnostic, he must protest the assumption that Christians are better regarded by the Creative Spirit than other humans. Such an assumption is based on the belief in a God with human shortcomings, a God who created billions of human beings before sending his Son to earth to redeem humanity and who excluded all those billions of human beings from future bliss. This view is a sort of religious racism, creating a privileged class of humanity for all eternity. What should one think of a heaven from which the majority of aspiring souls are excluded through no fault of their own? And what should one think of the Mormons, who baptize the dead ancestors of their members for their postmortem admission into the club?

For the Agnostic, the Creator is pure intelligence, not a human being with a little brain, a callous heart, enormously presumptuous and of little sensitivity. It is a spirit, a part of which stirs within us, a spirit which human language is inadequate to express.

A Christian lives with guilt; life itself has arisen from sensual desire—and so sinful; all of mankind owes its existence

167

to the original sin committed by Adam and Eve in the Garden. Christian preachers foster this guilt feeling; it is emphasized from the pulpit and in Christian theological writings. One of the famous chants in Latin medieval liturgy is the *Dies Irae,* which refers to the Day of Judgment in the following terms:

> Dies irae, dies illa
> Solvet saeclum in favilla.
> Iudex ergo cum sedebit,
> Nil inultum remanebit . . .

> The day of wrath, that day
> Will consume the age in ashes,
> Whatever hidden, will appear,
> Nothing will remain unpunished.

To still further increase the anguish of the audience, the chant adds:

> Quid sum miser tunc dicturus,
> Quem patronem rogaturus
> Cum vix justus sit securus?

> What shall I, miserable, say then,
> Which protector shall I then invoke,
> When even the Just will not feel safe?

Crushed by guilt feeling, a Christian devout will need the priest, to absolve him of his sins. No matter what he does, he will never be able to wash his soul clean. He will have this impure earthly existence over with, leave this "Valley of Misery" as soon as possible to enjoy the unsullied bliss of Paradise.

In the eyes of the Agnostic, man is guilty only if he commits acts harmful to society, to other people, or to himself. The Agnostic has no feeling of guilt and can live serenely. The Agnostic does not despise the flesh, but enjoys what nature offers him. Spirit and flesh are interrelated. Anatole France makes the Abbé Coignard say, "I wish for a good book and a good meal." The Abbé, as a character, is a worthy successor to Rabelais.

The idea for an Agnostic is to achieve a synthesis of the flesh and of the mind for the purpose of truly and nobly enjoying life.

THE ENIGMA OF THE UNIVERSE

For the Agnostic, the enigma of the universe consists of this: nature is indifferent to the fate of the individual. The species has a better chance of surviving, but even if a whole group disappears, nature will remain insensible of the fact. Life will continue in one way or another in the universe. Many species that once lived on this planet are now extinct; others have taken their place. The preservation of life is incumbent upon the living. Everything dies, but life unceasingly fights death with enormous vitality. Sure to succumb in the end, life nevertheless maintains itself throughout innumerable vicissitudes.

Life is freedom, death is determinism. The Cosmos exhibits a harmony of contradiction, freedom within determinism. The infinite wisdom of this grand design is everywhere manifest in nature. Its author imparted his own essence to his work. Is this all there is, or is this essence of creation both inside and outside of the work?

We see nothing outside nature, outside the Cosmos. We only perceive the Cosmos. Existence outside the Cosmos is an abstraction, made by man, who has learned to create many abstractions.

Religion, philosophy offer sometimes converging, sometimes diverging answers to these questions. The agnostic answer is the most succinct, the most unequivocal, and the least presumptuous. It consists of one word, one delectable word that Michel de Montaigne inscribed on the ceiling of his study. This word is *Nescio,* Latin for "I do not know," a word expressing not indifference, but humility and awe; not defeat, but acceptance of the enigma.

In his drama *Faust,* the result of more than 60 years of work, Goethe gives a similar answer, which is couched in beautiful, poetic language. Gretchen, an innocent young girl, very much in love with Faust, instinctively feels that there is something she does not understand about her "lover" in regard to religion. She questions him:

Margaret: Do you believe in God?

Faust: My dear, who dares to say:
I believe in God?
Question any priest or philosopher,
And his answer will seem to mock you.

Margaret: So you don't believe?

Faust: Don't misunderstand me, my love.
Who dares to name him?
Who can declare:
I believe in him?
Does not the all-encompassing,
the all-supporting,
embrace and uphold us,
you, me and Himself?
Does not the sky arch over us?
When we gaze in each other's eyes,
is there not a surging in your heart and head,
formed by the eternal mystery,
invisibly and visibly about you!
Fill your great heart with that,
and when you're wholly overcome by the feeling,
then call it what you will:
call it joy, or heart, or love, or God!
I have no name for it!
Feeling is everything;
the name is sound and smoke
beclouding the glow of heaven.[1]

The above can be regarded as the conclusion and last word of the Agnostic.

NOTES

Chapter I. The Balance Sheet of Religion

[1]See any book or encyclopedia on Greek mythology.
[2]Saint Augustine, *The City of God,* pp. 203–204.
[3]"Catholicism," in the collection *The Great Religions of Modern Man* (New York: Braziller).
[4]Saint Augustine, *The City of God,* Book XIV, p. 441.
[5]Saint Augustine, *The Confessions of . . .,* Book I, Chapter 7.
[6]Mona Abousenna, *Los Angeles Times,* Dec. 16, 1982.
[7]G. Faigniez, ed., Documents relatifs àl'histoire du commerce et de l'industrie en France. Quoted by Eileen Power in *Medieval People* (Garden City, NY: Doubleday & Co., 1954).
[8]See Rilliet, Calvin and Servetus.
[9]Dante, *The Divine Comedy,* Canto III, verses 1–9.

Chapter II. Reflections on the Book of Genesis

[1]In the Babylonian myth of the Flood, the counterpart of Noah is Utanapishtim, a servant of the god Ea, who decided to save mankind while the other gods had resolved to destroy it by flood. This Babylonian Noah constructed a ship under the instruction of his master, taking into it his family, his gold and silver, domestic and wild animals, and men skilled in navigation to cope with the dangers of the voyage and of disembarkation. The rain lasted for six days and six nights; on the seventh day the storm abated. The floods had carried the ship to the summit of Mount Nisir. (See Robert Aton, *The God of the Beginnings,* New York: William Morrow & Co., 1966, p. 56.) The authors—probably Greek-speaking Jews—borrowed the Bible story from Babylonian sources or from Greek mythology.

Lloyd M. Graham, in his book *Deceptions and Myths of the Bible* (New York: Bell Publishing Co., p. 101), gives a list of the cultures in which the story of the Deluge can be found, with the names of the hero who, like Noah, was warned by the God to construct a ship in order to save himself and his family, and to take animals into his ship with which to repopulate the earth. The names of the gods, allies of man, also are given.

Sir Leonard Woolley (Aron, p. 115), leader of a seven-year Anglo-American archeological expedition at Ur in Mesopotamia, believed he had found proof of the occurrence of the Flood. The excavations he conducted between 1927 and 1929 in a prehistoric cemetery led to the discovery of a great quantity of rubble from the primitive city. Shafts sunk in the spring of 1929 uncovered a layer of charred wood and clay tablets, which allowed the dating of Ur's lost civilization. As the shafts went deeper, the character of the soil changed, as did the discoveries: No more rubble and tablets, but a homogeneous eight-foot-deep layer of clay, devoid of any extraneous elements. In the rubble below the clay were found shards of pottery, bricks, and flint tools whose shape and materials bore witness to an advanced civilization dating as far back as 3000 B.C. However, this finding does not necessarily prove the occurrence of the Flood, or the Deluge that figures in the myths of so many prehistoric nations. The soil of Ur might have been soaked by subterranean water or by local and frequent rainfalls.

[2]Simpson, *The Meaning of Evolution,* p. 5.

Chapter III. Of God and Man

[1]Saint Augustine, *Sermo CCXLI.* Quoted in "Catholicism," *The Great Religions of Modern Man,* pp. 29, 30.

Chapter IV. God and the Philosophers

[1]Plato, *The Republic,* Book VII.
[2]Aristotle, *Metaphysics,* Book XII, Chapter 6.
[3]Ibid., p. 34.
[4]Ibid., p. 35.
[5]Ibid.
[6]Ibid.
[7]Strem, *The Life and Teaching of Lucius Annaeus Seneca,* p. 158.
[8]Lucretius, "Of the Nature of Things," in the collection *The World's Great Thinkers,* p. 14.
[9]*Novum Organum,* CXVI.
[10]Francis Bacon, "Of Atheism," in *Essays and the New Anlantis,* p. 16.
[11]*Novum Organum,* LXV.
[12]Ibid.

[13]Ibid.

[14]Pascal, "Pensées," in the collection *The World's Great Thinkers,* p. 20.

[15]Ibid., p. 34.

[16]Spinoza, *The Road to Inner Freedom,* in the chapter "The God That Is."

[17]Goethe, *Faust, Prologue in Heaven,* translation by Philip Wayne.

[18]See the chapter on Spinoza in Durant, *The Story of Philosophy.*

[19]Descartes, *Dictionary,* p. 72 (Burman, V. 169).

[20]Ibid., p. 75 (Cogitationes Privatae, x.218).

[21]Ibid., (Replies, x.87).

[22]Immanuel Kant, *Werke II,* quoted by Kung, p. 773.

[23]Carr, *Leibniz,* p. 96.

[24]Ibid., p. 25.

[25]Pomeau, *La Religion de Voltaire,* p. 171.

[26]Herbert Scheit, *Zum Verhältnis der Religion und der Gemeinde,* pp. 252–258.

[27]Ibid. Scheit quotes Hegel as follows: "The Jews cannot arrive at any beautiful social relationship, at objective freedom, because they feel themselves to be the property of an all-powerful Creditor. Because they are the total, serving property of their God, all their relations have been lacking a soul. Their God, that inspires fear or respect, is the expression of their self-consciousness in this way: for them exists only the principle of being ruled through the law, pre-ordained, not given to them by the people themselves, because the latter have no need for freedom. Their religious slavery led them to a purely animal existence, aiming at mere survival, eating and sex." And Hegel warned against complete renunciation of human freedom, complete abandon to the worship of the Absolute, citing the fate of the Jews as a deterrent.

Scheit (pp. 70–71) further quotes Hegel as saying: "The Jews reject Jesus, because these poor people, in the consciousness of their wretchedness, are opposed to Jesus who represents an intermediary between the human and the divine, and they, in their enslavement, in the consciousness of their impossibility of bridging the gap between the human and the Absolute, cannot fathom the relationship between the Son and the Father."

[28]Einstein, *Out of My Later Years,* p. 28.

[29]Ibid., p. 26.

[30]*The Philosophy of Schopenhauer,* p. 303.

[31]Ibid., p. 331.

[32]Bergson, *Evolution Créatrice,* p. 273.

[33]Bergson, *The Two Sources of Morality and Religion,* p. 92.

[34]Ibid.

[35]Sartre, *L'Existentialisme est un Humanisme*, p. 19.

[36]*Dialogues of Alfred North Whitehead,* recorded by Lucien Price, p. 296.

Chapter V. Of Good and Evil

[1]Solzhenitsyn, *The Gulag Archipelago,* p. 564.

Chapter VII. The Creed of an Agnostic

[1]Goethe, *Faust,* Part I., "Martha's Garden." Translated by C. F. MacIntyre (New Directions Paperbook No. 70).

BIBLIOGRAPHY

Aristotle. *On Man and the Universe.* Published for the Classics Club by Walter J. Black, New York.

Aron, Robert. *The God of the Beginnings.* New York: William Morrow and Co., 1966.

Bacon, Francis. "Novum Organum." In the collection *The World's Great Thinkers (The Philosophers of Science).* New York: Random House.

Bergson, Henri. *The Two Sources of Morality and Religion.* New York: Henry Holt & Co.

Bible. The Book of Genesis.

Boodin, John Elof. *God and Creation. Three Interpretations of the Universe.* New York: The Macmillan Co., 1934.

Bouman. *Gott und Mensch im Koran, Strukturform religiöser Anthropologie.* Darmstadt: Wissenschaftliche Buchgesellschaft, 1977.

Brantly, George, ed. "Catholicism." In the collection *Great Religions of Modern Man.* New York: George Braziller.

Bucke, Richard Maurice. *Cosmic Consciousness.* Dutton & Co.

Carr, Herbert Wildon. *Leibniz.* New York: Dover Publications.

Dante, Alighieri. *The Divine Comedy.* Translated by Lawrence Binyon. Penguin ("The Portable Dante." revised.)

Descartes. *Dictionary.* Translated and edited by John Morris. New York: Philosophical Library.

Durant, Will. *The Story of Philosophy.* New York: Simon and Schuster, 1953.

Einstein, Albert. In *Living Philosophies.* New York: World Publishing Co.

Goethe, Johann Wolfgang von. *Faust,* Part I. Translated by C. F. MacIntyre. New York: New Directions.

Goethe, Johann Wolfgang von. *Faust,* Part II. Translated by Philip Wayne. Penguin Classics.

Graham, Lloyd. *Deceptions and Myths of the Bible.* New York: Bell Publishing Co., 1979.

Hertzberg, Arthur, ed. "Judaism." In the collection *Great Religions of Modern Man.* New York: George Braziller, 1962.

Kant, Immanuel. *From Critique of Pure Reason.* In the collection *The World's Great Thinkers (Speculative Philosophers).* New York: Random House.

Kant, Immanuel. Presented by Julien Benda in the collection *The Living Thoughts Library.* Philadelphia: David McKay Co.

Kierkegaard, Svren. *Sick Unto Death.* Garden City, NY: Doubleday.

Koran. Le Koran qui est la guidance et le différenciateur, traduction litterale et compléte des sourates essentielles par le Dr. J. C. Mardrus, Paris. Eugéne Fasquelle, éditeur, 1926.

Koran. An explanatory translation by Mohammed Marmaduke Pickthall. Mentor Religious Classic.

Kung, Hans. *Does God Exist?* Translated by Edward Quinn. New York: Vintage Books.

Lucretius. *Of the Nature of Things.* In the collection *The World's Great Thinkers (Man and the Universe).* New York: Random House.

Malraux, André. *La Métamophose Des Dieux.* Nouvelle Revue Francaise. La Galerie de la Pléiade, Paris.

Masson, Denise. *Monothéisme Coranique et Monothéisme Biblique.* Paris: Etudes Comparsés, Desclee de Brouwer, 1976.

Montaigne, Michel de. *The Essays of Montaigne.* Translated by George B. Ives. New York: The Heritage Press.

Pascal, Blaise. "Pensees." In the collection *The World's Great Thinkers. (Speculative Philosophers).*

Plato. "The Republic." In *Five Great Dialogues.* New York: Walter J. Black.

Pomeau, Rene. *La Religion de Voltaire.* Paris: Librairie Nizet, 1966.

Price, Lucien. *Dialogues of Alfred North Whitehead.* New American Library.

Rilliet, Albert. *Calvin and Servetus.* London: Johnston, 1846.

Saint Augustine. *The Confessions.* Translated by Rex Warner. New American Library.

Saint Augustine. *The City of God.* New York: The Modern Library.

Sartre, Jean-Paul. *Existentialisme est un Humanisme.* Paris: Nagel.

Scheit, Herbert. *Geist und Gemeinde, zum Verhältnis der Religion und Politik bei Hegel.* München: Pustel.

Schopenhauer, *The Philosophy of Schopenhauer.* New York: Modern Library.

Simpson, George Gaylord. *The Meaning of Evolution.* New Haven, CT: Yale University Press, 1950.

Solzhenitsyn, Alexander. *The Gulag Archipelago.* New York: Harper & Row.

Spinoza, Baruch. *The Road to Inner Freedom, the Ethics.* New York: Philosophical Library.

Stickelberger, Emmanuel. *Calvin, a Life.* John Knox & Bros., 1961.

Strem, George. *The Life and Teaching of Lucius Annaeus Seneca.* Vantage Press, 1981.

INDEX

177

DATE DUE

NOV - 3			
MAR 0 9 2012			
GAYLORD			PRINTED IN U.S.A.